ADHD COACHING MATTERS

THE DEFINITIVE GUIDE

ADHD
COACHING
MATTERS

— *the* —

definitive
guide

SARAH D. WRIGHT

Every attempt has been made to make this book as accurate and complete as possible. However there may be mistakes, both typographical and in content. Furthermore, some of the information contained in this book consists of website references that are current only up to the printing date.

The material presented in this book is intended for informational purposes only. It should be considered neither an endorsement, nor a substitute for your own judgment as to what training program, certification, and course of action is best for you.

ACO Books
An imprint of the ADHD Coaches Organization
College Station, TX

To request permission to reuse information in this book, contact ACOBooks.com

Library of Congress Cataloging-in-Publication Data
Wright, Sarah D., 1958-
ADHD coaching matters: the definitive guide / Sarah D. Wright.
pages cm
Includes glossary, bibliographical references and index.
ISBN-13: 978-0692205266 (pbk.)
ISBN-10: 0692205268 (pbk.)
1. Psychology & counseling. 2. Attention-deficit & attention-deficit-hyperactivity disorder. 3. Business development. I.Title.
Library of Congress Control Number: 2014908005

Edited by Megan Hoover
Book design by Vansuka Chindavijak

"Sarah Wright has done the impossible! As a founding board member of the ADHD Coaches Organization and ten-year veteran as a certified ADHD Coach, I am amazed that in one book, Wright has taken twenty years of ADHD Coaching history and captured every salient detail. What a valuable wealth of information. And all at your fingertips! *ADHD Coaching Matters: The Definitive Guide*, is a true masterpiece that could only have been written by someone with Wright's unique professional experience with ADHD Coaching. As a trainer and mentor coach for new and emerging coaches, I will definitely be recommending this book as a "must-read' resource, again and again!"—*Laurie Dupar, PMHNP, RN, PCC*

"Wow! This book is just what the ADHD Coaching community needs! Sarah Wright—a true pioneer and leader in the field—has written a compact, well-researched guide for those new to the field as well as seasoned professionals. She covers everything from where to get training to where to get insurance, and includes the history of coaching, a clear explanation of what ADHD Coaching is, and a discussion of relevant research. As a proponent of coaching from the beginning, I know it is often difficult to explain the value of coaching to other professionals, and even to clients. This guide fills that void. A must-have for those in the ADHD coaching community. You might even want to give a copy to a physician or two..." —*Michele Novotni, PhD Psychologist, ADHD Coach, Past President ADDA*

"Almost every day at ADDitude we hear 'How can I find an ADHD Coach?' People with ADHD need coaching, but ADHD Coaches are few in number. Sarah D. Wright's welcome addition to the coaching literature clarifies clearly and comprehensively what ADHD Coaching is and explains the training and certification process. With extensive experience as an ADHD Coach, Wright is uniquely qualified as the person to inspire a new generation of sorely-needed ADHD Coaches." —*Susan Caughman, Editor-in-Chief, ADDitude*

"This guidebook is a gem! Sarah D. Wright provides an inside look at ADHD Coaching and credentialing, demystifying options for coaches in a clear, concise, well-researched book. A must read, not only for people considering becoming an ADHD Coach, but for anyone interested in ADHD Coaching." —*Jodi Sleeper-Triplett, MCC, SCAC, BCC*

"A book like this has been begging to be written. And Sarah D. Wright was exactly the right person to have answered the call. With her long and multifaceted history in the field of ADHD Coaching, she brings the consummate insider's view to what has become one of the most important disciplines in the coaching profession—that of helping people with ADD/ADHD live to their potential. Speaking as someone who had to find his own way through the process of becoming a trained ADHD Coach, I can attest to this book's immense value for anyone interested, or already ensconced, in this noble profession." —*Alan Brown, creator of ADD CrusherTM Videos & Tools*

"Over the last 20 years, ADHD Coaches have proven to be invaluable resources for many of my patients with ADHD, helping them set goals and achieve success. It's now time to turn the tables and provide an invaluable resource for anyone thinking about pursuing this exciting helping career. *ADHD Coaching Matters: The Definitive Guide* is that book! Written by Sarah D. Wright, an author and coach since 2002, this first-of-its-kind book offers background and advice from a seasoned expert and leader in the field. Packed with information about the development of the profession as well as resources for ADHD Coach training and certification, this comprehensive guidebook is destined to become the source book for ADHD Coaches!" —*Patricia O. Quinn, MD*

"*ADHD Coaching Matters: The Definitive Guide* is one of the most important books you will ever own to use on your ADHD Coaching journey. Are you looking for a well-established ADHD Coach training program as a first step towards becoming an ADHD Coach? Are you already a trained ADHD Coach seeking out certification to establish yourself as an elite in the field of ADHD Coaching? Are you a trained Life Coach wanting to pursue ADHD Coaching? This is the book for you! Sarah D. Wright has done a phenomenal job in putting together a wealth of information that will educate you about the ADHD Coaching profession. Looking back on my own journey in becoming the first trained and certified ADHD Coach in Denmark, this book would have saved me a lot of time, energy, and money!" —*Charlotte Hjorth, PCC, PCAC, ACCG, PACG*

"It's scary that anyone can call themselves an ADHD Coach. How can you tell the competent professional ADHD Coaches from those who are simply co-opting the name? Thank goodness for Sarah D. Wright! This book is yet another example of how she is leading our industry by educating coaches, the ADHD community, and the public about the profession of ADHD Coaching. This guidebook tells you how to become a professional ADHD Coach—a coach who knows what they are doing, who is trained in best practices, and who abides by ethical standards. If you have any interest in becoming, hiring, or collaborating with an ADHD Coach, this book belongs in your library." —*Jeff Copper, Professional Certified ADHD Coach, founder and host of the Attention Talk Network*

"Sarah D. Wright, of all the professionals I know, has the understanding, wisdom and experience to write this book. She has never failed to impress me with her depth of knowledge and understanding of ADHD and what it takes to transform the life of someone with this brain type through ADHD Coaching. Wright has played a major leadership role in the ADHD Professional Community and this book will prove to be an invaluable resource for anyone interested in learning more about this rewarding profession." —*Carol Gignoux, MEd*

"This book is a much needed addition to the field that will make it much easier for new (and established) ADHD Coaches to learn the lay of the land. Sarah D. Wright has done the painstaking work of bringing together all of the practical matters of coaching that are important but not easy to find, such as the various options for training and certification, what the different credentials mean, and how to get liability insurance. She also provides valuable history and discusses the people who shaped it—this is not just interesting, but also gives important context to the current state of the field. If you are serious about being an ADHD Coach, you need to read this book." —*Ari Tuckman, PsyD, MBA*

"The wealth of information Sarah D. Wright has researched and compiled within the pages of this comprehensive reference makes it easy to endorse it as the Definitive Guide to ADHD Coaching Matters. Having been there since the beginning, I can testify that it's really all here! And organized and designed in an ADHD and dyslexic-friendly way, making it extremely easy for anyone to find what they are looking for. It belongs on the bookshelves of anyone remotely associated with ADHD: coaches, parents, partners, teachers, doctors, mental health professionals, and anyone looking for a coach." —*Madelyn Griffith-Haynie, multi-certified coaching pioneer, co-founder of the profession of ADHD Coaching and founder of the field of ADHD Coach Training*

"No one in the world is as well suited to explain ADHD Coaching as cogently and comprehensively as Sarah D. Wright. Sarah has a unique perspective informed by her experiences as a former scientist, engineer, manager, and corporate executive, and current professional ADHD Coach and leader in the ADHD Coaching community for more than a decade. Sarah matches her vast experience with an incisive, analytical mind. The result is a thoroughness to her explanation of "ADHD Coaching Matters" that is unparalleled—and long overdue." —*Elaine Taylor-Klaus, CPCC, ACC*

"ADHD Coaching has been a promising intervention for adults with ADHD but has been largely hampered by a lack of consensus as to its practices and the credentials needed for its practitioners. This book describes the growing consensus among professional ADHD Coaches for a certain set of practices, a concise definition of those practices, the evidence for them, and the credentials necessary to practice them. I highly recommend this book for anyone considering or currently practicing ADHD Coaching or those interested in better understanding this intervention." —*Russell A. Barkley, Ph.D., Clinical Professor of Psychiatry and Pediatrics at the Medical University of South Carolina in Charleston*

"What a great resource! Sarah D. Wright has researched the history of ADHD Coaching and collected descriptions of all of the ADHD Coach training and certification options available in the world. If anyone wants to know what ADHD Coaching is all about and how and where to get trained, *ADHD Coaching Matters: The Definitive Guide* is your one stop shop. Sarah even gives you the contact information in order to find out more. This book is the place to start on your journey to become an ADHD Coach. I'll be recommending it to anyone I come in contact with who is interested in ADHD Coaching." —*Alan R Graham, PhD, PCC, SCAC, MCAC, Dean of the MentorCoach ADHD Training Program*

"In any profession, knowing its history provides perspective, continuity, and cohesiveness. This book provides us with that history, as well as a rich trove of additional information about professional ADHD Coaching that anyone interested in this topic will want to read. It will serve for years to come as both as a reference for every current and future ADHD Coach, and as a milestone in the development of the profession of ADHD Coaching." —*Nancy Ratey, MCC, MEd*

"Everyday, fresh brain insights encourage a more comprehensive approach for both improved ADHD diagnostic precision and ADHD treatment predictability. These new data provide increasingly complex answers that specifically embrace brain and biomedical realities repeatedly found in those who suffer with Executive Function difficulties. ADHD Coaches bring these neuroscience applications down to street levels that add utilitarian value for both medical teams and those who suffer with ADHD. As a medical professional with considerable experience working with ADHD Coaches, I strongly urge everyone in the ADHD community—at every level—to use ADHD Coaching Matters as a guide for team building and improved ADHD medical care." —*Dr. Charles Parker, MD*

"Sarah D. Wright has written an important book for the ADHD community. *ADHD Coaching Matters: The Definitive Guide* is the only place one will find all this information on ADHD Coaching. I recommend ADHD Coaching to most of my clients as part of their treatment protocol, but there is little information out there that answers all the questions a potential client might have. For those looking to enter the field of ADHD Coaching, this book also explains what ADHD Coaching is, how and where to get trained, and also offers up a deep understanding of the history of ADHD Coaching. I am so glad to have this on my reference shelf!" —*Terry Matlen, MSW, Author of "Survival Tips for Women with ADHD" and "The Queen of Distraction", and Founder/director of ADDconsults.com*

"Looking for the ADHD Coach training that's right for you? Sarah D. Wright, founding board member of the ADHD Coaches Organization, has done the work for you. This comprehensive guide to ADHD Coach training and certification is the only book of its kind. Maybe you are just beginning to look into becoming an ADHD Coach, or maybe you are already an ADHD Coach and want to further your knowledge. In either case, this book is the roadmap that will help you find the training or certification that's right for you." —*Joyce Kubik, CMC, ADHD Coaches Organization President*

"How incredible to see the stunning response to the needs, potential, and value of people with ADHD as shown by the wealth of ADHD Coach training efforts reported in this book. Thanks to Sarah D. Wright for pulling together the full vision of our commitment." —*Denslow Brown, MCC, CPO, CPO-CD*

TABLE OF
CONTENTS

FOREWORD

Professional and Personal Coaching have been in existence for several decades, but only in the last twenty years has there been recognition that coaching those with Attention Deficit Hyperactivity Disorder requires special skills and proper training.

ADHD Coaching Matters: The Definitive Guide provides the reader with a clear definition of ADHD Coaching and clarifies what is required to become an ADHD Coach. This book eliminates the confusion on how ADHD Coaching differs from both skills coaching and from life coaching, and why those differences are important for the success of the person with ADHD. In this book, Sarah D. Wright has also accurately recounted the development of this specialty profession, and provided a comprehensive reference for all who wish to understand this rapidly growing and highly rewarding field.

The publication of *ADHD Coaching Matters* is also timely. This is an exciting time for ADHD Coaching, as research on its efficacy as a supportive process is beginning to emerge. Testimonial support for ADHD Coaching existed at least a decade before empirical peer reviewed studies began to appear, and research is now available that supports ADHD Coaching as beneficial. You can learn about the current research in this book.

There has never been any doubt in my mind as to how useful my ADHD Coaching services have been to the multitude of people with whom I have worked over the years who are affected by ADHD, yet there has always been regret that there are so many people to help and so few coaches to help them.

This is changing.

More professionals are interested in adding ADHD Coaching to the services they provide, and more postsecondary students are expressing interest in becoming ADHD Coaches. This book is a resource that will provide direction for all those interested in becoming a trained and certified ADHD Coach.

As with all emerging fields, there is still much work to be done. The existing—and expanding—demand for ADHD Coaches needs to be met, and there are improvements to be made in both knowledge base and coaching models.

It is my hope that this book stimulates and directs both the interest of those already in—or studying to be in—the helping professions, and those researchers and academics whose field of interest is ADHD, to learn more about ADHD Coaching.

It is only by the expansion of research and knowledge, and the sharing of experiences, that ADHD Coaching will continue to improve in quality and expand to meet the growing need.

This book will help make that happen.

Sandy Maynard, MS
Catalytic Coaching
Washington, DC

PREFACE

ADHD Coaching was introduced to the world on March 15th 1994 with the publication of the seminal book, *Driven to Distraction*[1], in which coaching for people with ADHD was first mentioned in print. The ideas expressed in that book were not created out of whole cloth, but were based on the real-life experiences of people like Nancy Ratey and Sue Sussman, who were already beginning to develop these techniques.

At that time, ADHD was still largely thought of as a disorder of childhood. The books *Driven to Distraction* and *You Mean I'm not Lazy, Stupid or Crazy?!*[2] were just beginning to change that perception. So much of what we know now about ADHD was yet to be learned.

The same was true of life coaching. There were just a handful of life coach training programs, and little in the way of consensus, not to mention research, regarding the definition, practice, and efficacy of life coaching.

Much has changed in twenty years.

As a founding board member of the ADHD Coaches Organization (ACO), where I have served for the better part of a decade, I have been in a particularly good position to both observe and participate in the evolution of the ADHD Coaching profession.

Both my coaching career and my work at the ACO have been informed by my prior experiences as an academic, scientist, engineer, manager, and corporate executive. Since starting my ADHD Coach training at the Optimal Functioning Institute in 2002, because of my interests and background, I have thought about and debated key issues with colleagues, looked for and read relevant research, talked with many people about ADHD and coaching, collected and analyzed all sorts of information, and written and presented on what I thought was important for the ADHD Coaching profession.

As the years went on, those of us on the Board of Directors of the ACO continued to be plagued by a particular question: What exactly *is* ADHD Coaching? The profession has for a long time had a clear definition of what an ADHD Coach is (a trained life coach with additional training and expertise in working with people affected by ADHD), but not of what ADHD Coaching is. Our ability to fulfill the ACO's mission of promoting ADHD Coaches and Coaching worldwide could not be met without being able to articulate clearly what ADHD Coaching is.

Additionally, a clear definition of ADHD Coaching is necessary so that members of the general public know what to expect when they hire an ADHD Coach. A definition is necessary to determine whether a practitioner is doing ADHD Coaching or something else (for example, educational therapy or psychotherapy using some coaching techniques). Finally, a definition is necessary so that it can be tested by research and thereby confidently recommended as an effective process that helps people affected by ADHD begin to lead the lives they wish to have.

By 2012, two groups of dedicated coaches had gone through the thoughtful, intensive, laborious effort of creating an ADHD Coaching certification. Although both described ADHD Coaching and defined clear ADHD Coaching competencies and the means to test them, neither had presented the profession with a concise, evidence-based definition of ADHD Coaching.

Recognizing the critical need for this definition—one that codified the essential elements of ADHD Coaching as it is now understood to be after 20 years of experience and research—the board of the ACO invited all the leaders in the field to participate in a Thought Leader Summit to help create such a definition for the ACO. This turned out to be an extraordinary conversation that revealed a broad consensus of the elements that must be present for an interaction between practitioner and client to be considered ADHD Coaching. The ACO's definition of ADHD Coaching that grew out of that summit, and the evidence base for it, is discussed in this book.

At the beginning of 2013, knowing that the most frequently asked question on the ACO's help line is: "How do I become an ADHD Coach?" Joyce Kubik requested that I present on ADHD Coach training and certification at the upcoming conference, which I did. Later, she suggested that I write this book, which I also did.

So, on the 20th anniversary of the birth of ADHD Coaching, this guidebook provides you with everything you might need to know about ADHD Coaching and how to become an ADHD Coach. It is filled with information about the history of the profession, the people and organizations involved, discussion of what ADHD Coaching is and isn't, an introduction to pertinent research, the current training and certification options, options for obtaining liability insurance, and more.

I hope you find it both interesting and useful.

Sarah D. Wright
March 15, 2014
San Diego, CA

ACKNOWLEDGMENTS

This book would not have been possible without the experience and expertise of the many hundreds of ADHD Coaches whose dedication has driven them to cumulatively acquire hundreds of thousands of hours of experience coaching people affected by ADHD. It is this real world experience, coupled with research and evidence-based practices—in this and related fields—that has been distilled into the information and resources in this guidebook.

I thank the teachers whose expertise, dedication, and leadership inspire the next generation of instructors and ADHD Coaches on a daily basis.

I thank the visionaries at the Institute for the Advancement of ADHD Coaching and at the Professional Association of ADHD Coaches for going through the arduous process of creating a meaningful certification process for ADHD Coaches.

I thank my colleagues on the board of the ADHD Coaches Organization and all those who participated in, or contributed to, the 2013 Thought Leader Summit that was so pivotal in creating the definition of ADHD Coaching.

I thank Joyce Kubik, who first suggested that I give a conference presentation on ADHD Coach training and certification and later, that I write this book.

I thank Valerie English-Cooper who initiated and led the project that resulted in the ADHD Coaches Organization's 2013 Membership Survey.

The chapters on ADHD Coaching and the evidence for it benefited greatly from the expertise and attention of Elizabeth Ahmann, Virginia Hurley, and Sandy Maynard.

The chapters on certification and on the history of life and ADHD Coaching were made more accurate, detailed, and vivid by conversations and correspondence with C.J. Hayden, Madelyn Griffith-Haynie, Lisa Grossman, Barbara Luther, Sandy Maynard, David Matthew Prior, Nancy Ratey, Jodi Sleeper-Triplett, and Sue Sussman.

The book benefited greatly from the attention of two very knowledgeable editors. My sincere thanks go to Barbara Luther for contributing her significant experience and expertise to ensure the details were correct, and to Megan Hoover for her coaching and careful editing of the manuscript, notes, and citations. Thank you both for your time, effort, expertise, and passion for this project. I acknowledge any remaining mistakes as mine alone.

I thank my delightful and talented daughter, Rebecca, for her encouragement and support and the many hours she spent in helping me get this book to the finish line.

I thank my son, Danny, who inspired my career and is proud that his stories go out in the world and make a difference. I am proud of him too. He is a force for good in this world.

And finally, I thank Kevin, my partner in life and love, for his interest in this project, for the many conversations in which he helped me vet ideas, and for giving me the space and support I needed to get it all done.

DEDICATION

This book is dedicated to all those who have gone before: to the leaders, visionaries, teachers, mentors, researchers, and those living with ADHD who knew there had to be a better way. Coaching is the key to unlocking the great reservoir of potential that lies within each of us, and particularly in those with ADHD for whom, in the words of Ned Hallowell, "ADHD is a gift that is hard to unwrap."

EPIGRAPH

"We don't accomplish anything in this world alone... and whatever happens is the result of the whole tapestry of one's life and all the weavings of individual threads from one to another that creates something." —*Sandra Day O'Connor*

INTRODUCTION

01

This book was written to be a road map to the field of ADHD Coaching. With its help, readers interested in learning more about this profession can find their way to the answers they seek.

The book starts with an overview of the history of life coaching, followed by an overview of the history of ADHD Coaching. You will note as you read, that these two histories are intimately intertwined. If you want to learn more about the history of life coaching, you may want to read Vicki Brock's *Sourcebook of Coaching History.*[3]

Some readers will find this historical material intrinsically interesting. However, the purpose of these chapters is simply to help you get your bearings. The chapters introduce you to key events, personalities, organizations, and acronyms. This information becomes useful in the chapters on ADHD Coach training and certification where references to people, organizations, and acronyms abound.

The history chapters are followed by chapters on the definition of ADHD Coaching and the evidence for it. This is the definition that has emerged after 20 years of experience and research, and there is broad consensus in the field that these are the elements that must be present for an interaction between practitioner and client to be considered ADHD Coaching. The definition is accompanied by an introduction to the research that supports it.

Those first chapters provide you with important context, the lay of the land so-to-speak. Once you've read them, you will want to peruse the subsequent chapters on training, certification, and liability insurance and decide for yourself how you will navigate through this terrain.

To clarify, the material presented in the chapters on training, certification, and liability insurance is intended for informational purposes only, and should be considered neither an endorsement, nor a substitute for your own judgment as to what training program, certification, and course of action is best for you.

Please also remember that although every attempt has been made to make this book as accurate and complete as possible, there may be mistakes. If you do find errors, omissions, or dead links, please contact the publisher so the mistakes can be corrected in subsequent editions.

The penultimate chapter of this book presents the results of the 2013 Membership Survey of the ADHD Coaches Organization (ACO). This survey reflects the makeup of the ACO as of the first half of 2013, and by extension, the makeup of the profession as a whole at that time. In this chapter you can get an idea of who coaches are, where in the world they live, how they trained, how they coach, and more.

The final chapter takes a quick look back at where we've been and a quick look forward to where we might be going.

Additional resources include chronologies of the evolution of the profession, end notes, an index, and a glossary to help you decode credentials and other acronyms.

If you've read this far, you must have a serious intent to learn more about ADHD Coaching, and perhaps also to learn more about becoming an ADHD Coach. You are the reader this guidebook was written for. The following is your road map to the world of ADHD Coaching, coach training, and certification.

Enjoy the journey!

OVERVIEW OF THE HISTORY OF LIFE COACHING

02

The historical timeline for professional life coaching can be traced back to the 1930s, and beyond.[4] However, for our purposes, the timeline starts in the early 1970s when two influential events occurred. First, Werner Erhard developed and began teaching his *Erhard Seminars Training* (EST) at the Esalen Institute in California. EST later became *The Forum* and then *Landmark Education*.[5] Second, Timothy Gallwey, who was Erhard's tennis coach at the sports center at Esalen, published *The Inner Game of Tennis*.[6] According to O'Connor and Lages, the publication of this book was probably the start of life coaching as we know it, bringing together for the first time elements of humanistic psychology, Buddhist thinking, sports psychology, and the idea that individuals can affect their own subconscious.[7]

Vicki G. Brock, in her *Sourcebook of Coaching History*,[8] goes into depth regarding the influence of the Esalen Institute, Erhard, and Gallwey on the development of life coaching. In this overview, however, we will skip ahead to the early 1980s, when Thomas Leonard, generally recognized as the founder of life coaching, was Budget Director for Landmark Education.[9]

While at Landmark, Leonard became thoroughly familiar with the trainings and, integrating his diverse knowledge in finances and human potential psychology, began to work with people one-on-one to help them sort out not just their finances, but their lives. In 1988, Leonard started teaching his *Design Your Life* course and began collaborating with like-minded people including Laura Whitworth, Henry and Katherine Kimsey-House, Cheryl Richardson, Sandy Vilas, Pamela Richarde, and Madelyn Griffith-Haynie.[10]

In 1992 Thomas Leonard founded Coach University (now subsumed into CoachInc), and Laura Whitworth, who was his colleague at Esalen, co-founded the Coach Training Institute (CTI).[11] Many of the first generation of ADHD Coaches and coach trainers got their life coach training in one of these two programs.

In 1995, curious about how best to characterize this new thing they were doing, Laura Whitworth convened a coaches caucus in San Francisco, inviting the heads of coaching schools and other coach trainers, to attempt to define life coaching. In addition to Laura Whitworth, participants were Susan Berland, Breeze Carlile, Tony Gibbon, Barbara Gluck, C.J. Hayden, Frederic Hudson, Eric Kohner, Dorothy Largay, Cynthia Loy Darst, Roy Oster, David Peterson, David Matthew Prior, Nancy Ratey, Jeff Staggs, and Sue Sussman.[12]

The group came to the consensus that, despite their disparate backgrounds and training, there was a common core skill set they were using that was distinct from other professions. The outcome of this caucus was the first definition of life coaching and the formation of the Professional and Personal Coaches Association (PPCA).[13] The PPCA was a membership organization with dues, a code of ethics, and all the elements of a professional association.

Around the same time, Thomas Leonard founded the International Coach Federation (ICF) both as an alumni group for the graduates of Coach University[14] and a certification body for the profession.[15] In 1998 the ICF subsumed the PPCA, uniting the growing field of life coaching, and ICF became the organization that we are familiar with today.[16]

The ICF went on to become both the professional association and the certifying and accrediting body for the profession. Although other life coach certification bodies now exist, including the Center for Credentialing and Education (CCE), the International Association of Coaching (IAC), and two significant European-based organizations,[17] the ICF has been, and remains, the most recognized association for the life coaching profession.

In the 25 years since Thomas Leonard first offered his *Design Your Life* course, life coaching has taken off. There are now literally hundreds of life coach training schools. Of these, two are of particular relevance to the ADHD Coaching world, either because they now teach an ADHD Coaching specialty or because of their involvement in certifying coaches. The two schools are MentorCoach and the Institute for Life Coach Training.

MentorCoach was founded in 1997 by Ben Dean, PhD, MCC, to train individuals in the helping professions (psychologists, social workers, counselors, nurses, etc.) to become coaches. It is now one of the very few life coach training programs that offers an ADHD Coaching specialty.

In 1998, the Institute for Life Coach Training (ILTC) was founded by Pat Williams, PhD, MCC, who later collaborated with CCE to create the Board Certified Coach (BCC) certification that was launched in 2011.

By 2000, Thomas Leonard had left the ICF and begun evangelizing a new coaching paradigm. In the ensuing years he founded two new coaching schools—Coachville and the Graduate School of Coaching—and a new coaching association for certifying coaches, the International Association of Coaching (IAC).

Sadly, Thomas Leonard died in February 2003.

The IAC was formally launched in March 2003, a month after Leonard died. Like the other life coach certification organizations, it has a canon of core coaching skills, a code of ethics, and certification process. There is no special requirement for where or how coaches obtain knowledge and experience with the core skill set, only that they demonstrate they have it.

And finally, as mentioned above, CCE launched its Board Certified Coach (BCC) designation, developed in collaboration with Pat Williams, founder of the Institute for Life Coach Training, in 2011.

All of these certifications will be discussed further in the chapter on Life Coach Certification (chapter 7).

OVERVIEW OF THE HISTORY OF
03 ADHD COACHING

ADHD Coaching grew out of the specialized needs of the ADHD population, developing along its own path at the same time that life coaching was taking off in the general population. Three notable events occurred in 1994, making that the year we can say ADHD Coaching was born.

First, it was in March of 1994 that Hallowell and Ratey's seminal book, *Driven to Distraction*, was first published. It is in one of the final chapters of *Driven to Distraction*, in the chapter titled "What You Can Do About It," that the concept of ADHD Coaching makes its first appearance in print.[18] The ideas expressed in that book were based on the real-life experiences of Nancy Ratey and Sue Sussman, who were already beginning to develop these techniques.

That same year, Madelyn Griffith-Haynie, having developed a comprehensive curriculum specifically to train coaches to work with people affected by what was then called ADD, founded The Optimal Functioning Institute (OFI) and began training ADHD Coaches.[19] Subsequently, Sue Sussman and Nancy Ratey, who that same year founded the National Coaching Network (NCN) to be an ADHD Coach membership organization, began to formalize the skills they knew were working for their clients into a second ADHD Coach training program.[20]

Over the years, OFI proved to be of particular importance to the profession because it is where a significant number of former or current ADHD Coach trainers got their initial ADHD Coach training. These trainers include David Giwerc, Barbara Luther, Denslow Brown, Cameron Gott, Kate Kelly, Peggy Ramundo, and Lupita Volio.

In 1998, David Giwerc founded a third pivotal ADHD Coaching school, the ADD Coach Academy (ADDCA), which has since trained more ADHD Coaches than any other program. With its comprehensive approach, blending all the elements of ADHD Coaching into one integrated program, is often considered to be the gold standard for ADHD Coach training.

Also in 1998, Lisa Grossman and Karen Boutelle received their initial ADHD Coach training from Nancy Ratey.[21] Grossman took ADHD Coaching to Israel, where there is now a thriving ADHD Coach training and coaching community,[22] and Karen Boutelle went on to found the ADHD Coaching program at Landmark College in Putney, Vermont, the first such program in any post-secondary educational setting.

That was also the year that the NCN became the American Coaching Association (ACA) under Sussman's direction. The ACA continues to train ADHD Coaches, although Sussman now focuses on training life coaches through her FastTrack Academy program.[23]

In 2002, with ADHD Coaching gaining in popularity, the Attention Deficit Disorder Association (ADDA) formed a committee to develop a document that would clarify the principles of ADHD Coaching for both professionals and the general public. ADDA's Subcommittee on ADHD Coaching was chaired by Nancy Ratey and comprised by Linda Anderson, Victoria Ball, Ed Barniskis, Linda Barniskis, Sue Coleman, David Giwerc, Hope Langner, Mary Jane Johnson, Barbara Luther, Theresa Maitland, Jane Massengill, Sandy Maynard, Harold Meyer, Cynthia Runberg, Linda Sepe, Terrence Sole, and Sue Sussman.[24]

The result of the committee's efforts was *The ADDA Guiding Principles for Coaching Individuals with Attention Deficit Disorder.* This was the first attempt to codify ADHD Coaching and it reflects our earliest understanding of what ADHD Coaching is. You can still find that document online at NancyRatey.com.[25]

In 2003, the organization Children and Adults with Attention Deficit Hyperactivity Disorder (CHADD), posted a similar document, based largely on *The ADDA Guiding Principles for Coaching Individuals with Attention Deficit Disorder*, and posted it on their website. You can still find it there in their What We Know series of monographs.[26]

In 2004, Jodi Sleeper-Triplett founded a fourth pivotal ADHD Coach training program, focused on training life coaches to work with ADHD youth. This had not been done before, and now, ten years later, working with youth has become a significant segment of the profession.

OFI, ACA, ADDCA, and JST Coaching are landmark ADHD Coach training programs, which is why they are mentioned in this brief history of ADHD Coaching. These programs, and all the additional ADHD Coach training programs, are discussed in detail later in this guidebook.

In 2005, with a growing number of coaches specializing in working with people affected by ADHD, yet still lacking a true consensus as to what it means to be an ADHD Coach, the field of ADHD Coaching found itself in the same position as life coaching had been in a decade earlier.

That same year, two organizations with complementary missions—the ADHD Coaches Organization (ACO) and the Institute for the Advancement of ADHD Coaching (IAAC)—were formed to support the growing and specialized field of ADHD Coaching. Both defined ADHD Coaches to be trained life coaches first, with additional training and expertise in working with people affected by ADHD.

The ACO was formed as a membership association to promote community, excellence, education, and advocacy for the profession. The organization grew from a grassroots committee formed after the ADDA conference in May of 2005, and although many people were temporarily involved, the people who ultimately founded the organization were Glen Hogard and Ken Zaretzky, assisted by Cathy Jantzen. These three, along with Kerch McConlogue, Jan DeLaura, Laurie Dupar, and Sarah D. Wright, became the founding board members of the organization.

The IAAC was created to provide certification and ethical standards for the profession. The founders of this organization were Jodi Sleeper-Triplett, Sandy Maynard, Sue Sussman, Carol Gignoux, Linda Sepe, and Madelyn Griffith-Haynie. The IAAC developed the first industry standard certification for ADHD Coaches and began certifying coaches in 2009, certifying dozens of coaches before closing its doors in 2013. You will still see these certifications—Associate Certified ADHD Coach (ACAC), Certified ADHD Coach (CAC), and Senior Certified ADHD Coach (SCAC)—listed after many of their names.

In 2009, the Professional Association of ADHD Coaches (PAAC) was formed by Barbara Luther and Chana Klein, with a mission to establish high standards of excellence and to advocate for coaches and the profession of ADHD coaching, for the benefit of all individuals in need.[27] PAAC, which has strong connections to both ICF and ADDCA, began certifying ADHD Coaches in 2012 and is now the sole organization offering ADHD Coach certification.

In a continuing evolution of certification options, CCE, which provides certification, assessment, and management services to a large number of helping professions, collaborated with Pat Williams, founder of the Institute for Life Coach Training (ILCT), to create a Board Certified Coach (BCC) certification for life coaches which was launched in 2011.

In April of 2013, the ACO hosted a Thought Leader Summit, bringing together many of the most experienced coaches in the business. The purpose was, after almost 20 years of development and research, to identify the key elements of ADHD Coaching as it is now practiced. The goal of the summit was to develop a concise, empirically based, and research-supported definition of ADHD Coaching that could be used as a standard. The result of that crucial summit, and its broad consensus, can be found in the next chapter.

WHAT IS ADHD COACHING?

04

WHAT ADHD COACHING IS NOT

Before diving into the definition of ADHD Coaching—as it is understood to be after two decades of practice and research—it is helpful to briefly describe what it is not.

ADHD Coaching is not what most people are familiar with. It is not therapy, counseling, mentoring, training, teaching, managing, or consulting. It is also not advising, diagnosing, educational counseling, or tutoring.

All of those disciplines may use coaching techniques in their work, but they differ from ADHD Coaching in very important ways. Notably, in most helping professions, the practioner is considered an expert that the client is working with to improve or fix something about themselves.

In coaching, the philosophy is that there is nothing about the client that needs fixing, and the coach and client are colleagues, equal partners in focusing on and forwarding the client's agenda. Therefore, the coach does more asking than telling and more listening than talking, taking an evocative rather than didactic approach with the client.[28]

This is not to say that sharing of expertise, advising, educating, and problem analysis are not also, occasionally, part of ADHD Coaching. They are just not the primary purpose or approach.[29] And although learning and emotional healing may occur during coaching, the purpose of ADHD Coaching is neither to heal nor to teach. Instead, its purpose is to facilitate sustained change through self awareness, leading to the achievement of personal goals and optimal life satisfaction over time.[30]

SKILLS COACHING AND LIFE COACHING

There remains some confusion in the field of ADHD Coaching as to whether its focus is on improving skills and performance, or on helping clients to achieve their goals and dreams. In this book we use the terms *skills coaching* and *life coaching* as useful shorthand to distinguish between the two.

Skills coaching, as used here, refers to the process of helping another person to achieve or improve a particular behavioral performance. Skills coaching techniques are used by many professionals who have expertise in a particular area to impart that expertise to the person being coached. For example, skills coaching is employed by teachers, mentors, therapists, and coaches in many fields to help a student, client, patient, performer, or athlete improve his or her performance and competence. Skills coaching methods are derived primarily from a sports training model, and promote conscious awareness of resources and abilities and the development of conscious competence. This is the small 'c' coaching of Robert Dilts.[31]

In contrast to skills coaching, life coaching is a collaboration where client and coach are equal partners in focusing on and forwarding the client's agenda. The coaching is collaborative, client-centered, client-driven, and confidential. The coaching is focused on sustained cognitive, emotional, and behavioral changes that facilitate goal attainment, either in one's work or in one's personal life.[32] This is what Robert Dilts calls large 'C' coaching, and it emphasizes evolutionary change, concentrating on strengthening identity and values, and bringing dreams and goals into reality.[33]

SPECIAL CAVEAT FOR ADHD COACHES

It is important to note that ADHD, while still designated a mental health disorder,[34] is now known to be a genetically related, neurologically based brain difference (which, to provide some perspective, also describes left-handedness—another genetically related, neurologically based brain difference). That being said, psychological and physiological challenges such as anxiety, depression, and sleep disorders often co-occur with ADHD. This means that ADHD Coaches must be alert as to when to refer a client to other professionals for help with issues like anxiety, depression, medication, sleep, nutrition, exercise, etc. For coaching to be effective, clients must have addressed or be addressing their psychological and physiological health issues and be ready, willing, and able to participate in the coaching process.[35]

THE DEFINITION OF ADHD COACHING

Like all life coaching, ADHD Coaching addresses the needs and aspirations of the individual being coached. Importantly, ADHD Coaching also addresses the specific needs of clients who have ADHD or ADHD-like symptoms. ADHD Coaches therefore focus on working with clients on their personal goals and the pragmatic issues of achieving them while living with ADHD.

ADHD Coaching is a collaborative, supportive, goal-oriented process in which the coach and the client work together to identify the client's goals and then develop the self-awareness, systems, and strategies—the skills—necessary for the client to achieve those goals and full potential.

Because ADHD Coaching specifically addresses the needs of people affected by ADHD, it is a seamless blend of three elements employed by the coach as needed:

- Life Coaching: The client is regarded as an intact, creative, and resourceful person, and the coaching is collaborative, client-centered, client-driven, and confidential. The coach partners with the client in a thought-provoking and creative process to facilitate the client's actions toward self-awareness and achievement of the client's self-identified goals, providing structure and accountability, as needed, to help the client achieve those goals.

- Skills Coaching: The coach and client collaborate to develop conscious awareness of the client's strengths, challenges, and resources and, leveraging that awareness, develop conscious competence; creating systems and strategies tailored to the client's assets and environment that support and strengthen the client's ability to manage the pragmatic aspects of life.

- Education: The coach shares research-based information regarding aspects of Attention Deficit Hyperactivity Disorder and related topics relevant to the client's needs and interests. The coach may also offer information regarding tools, resources, and referrals as needed or requested by the client.

As will become even more evident in the next chapter, ADHD Coaching is necessarily more than simple life coaching, skills coaching, or education. The crux of ADHD

Coaching is using all three elements to help clients with the self-awareness required to understand and work with their own unique brains, thereby recognizing, appreciating, and using their strengths to reach their goals, enjoy their passions, and achieve lifelong well-being.

THE EVIDENCE FOR ADHD
05 # COACHING

For many years there was no direct evidence in support of ADHD Coaching. The ADHD Coach training programs were (and remain) proprietary, and any evidence for the efficacy of ADHD Coaching was borrowed from other disciplines.

As recently as 2005, Sam Goldstein, editor of the *Journal of Attention Disorders*, challenged the legitimacy of ADHD Coaching. He had done a literature search and failed to identify a single peer-reviewed or even quasi-scientific study or paper published during the previous 10 years on the topic of ADHD Coaching.[36]

Thankfully, that has changed. There is a growing body of research that speaks directly to the efficacy of ADHD Coaching, and its elements, as beneficial for people affected by ADHD. The following is an introduction to that research.

LIFE COACHING

Since 2005, the definition of ADHD Coaches is that they are trained life coaches first, with additional training and expertise in working with people affected by ADHD. Therefore, the first of the three elements of ADHD Coaching is life coaching.

As previously discussed, the aim of life coaching is sustained cognitive, emotional, and behavioral changes that facilitate goal attainment, either in one's work or in one's personal life.[37] Life coaching facilitates this by emphasizing evolutionary change, concentrating on strengthening identity and values, and bringing dreams and goals into reality.[38]

Sadly, people with ADHD have often experienced so much difficulty in their lives that they may have stopped believing that they *can* achieve their dreams, and may have even stopped dreaming. Cognitive coaching addresses clients' mental models,[39] and can be employed to help individuals with ADHD overcome their negativity and sense of failure. Evidence-based positive psychology approaches[40] are also b   nd beneficial in ADHD Coaching.

          kman, in his comprehensive, well-researched *   ntegrative Treatment for Adult ADHD: A Practical,   -To-Use Guide for Clinicians*, speaks of the powerful   ence of ADHD Coaching when he writes that coaching   what creates ADHD clients' success in the present, cutting "the chains of failure binding them to their pasts."[41]

Russell Barkley, perhaps the most prominent name in ADHD research, has been investigating the role of executive functioning in ADHD. He defines executive function to be: "the use of self-directed actions to choose goals, and to select, enact, and sustain actions across time toward those goals, usually in the context of others and often relying on social and cultural means. This is done for the maximization of one's longer-term welfare as the person defines that to be."[42]

Life coaching, therefore, would seem to be strongly supportive of executive function, and thus be of particular benefit to people affected by ADHD.

Life coaching is also the aspect of ADHD Coaching that inspires action. When the client has aspirations, they inspire the development of the skills in the present necessary to achieve those dreams in the future.

This leads to the second element of ADHD Coaching: the development of the self-awareness, systems, and strategies—the skills—that assist the client in managing the pragmatic aspects of life.

SKILLS COACHING

Because people affected by ADHD often struggle with what can be described as self-management, the second element of ADHD Coaching is, in part, the "development of the systems and strategies tailored to the client's assets and environment that support and strengthen the client's ability to manage the pragmatic aspects of life."

This element of ADHD Coaching focuses more on the process of helping the client to achieve or improve a particular behavioral performance, promoting conscious awareness of resources and abilities and the development of conscious competence.[43]

Skills coaching is what is described and recommended by Dawson and Guare in *Coaching Students with Executive Skills Deficits*.[44] It is also the kind of coaching recommended for ADHD by Hallowell and Ratey in *Driven to Distraction*,[45] and by Tuckman in his comprehensive treatment model. Tuckman's model includes family education as a clinical intervention, effective medication options, cognitive behavioral therapy for depression, anxiety, and self-esteem issues, and coaching for better life management. Of coaching, he writes, "it's the part that was missing from many of these clients' former therapies."[46]

Adult learning models[47] are often drawn upon in this aspect of ADHD Coaching, and the evidence-based program described by Safren et al. in *Mastering Your Adult ADHD*[48] is another example of behavioral-level interventions for ADHD symptoms.

Russell Barkley's research into executive function and ADHD highlights that the key to living well with ADHD is to design prosthetic environments around the individual to compensate for executive function deficits. This "scaffolding" includes externalizing information so that it is available at key points of performance, externalizing reminders and prompts related to tasks and deadlines, breaking up lengthy tasks into smaller clearly defined steps, and externalizing sources of problem solving and motivation.[49]

Designing these specific prosthetic environments is exactly what an ADHD Coach does when employing this element of ADHD Coaching where, as defined above, "The coach and client collaborate to develop conscious awareness of the client's strengths, challenges, and resources and, leveraging that awareness, develop conscious competence; creating systems and strategies tailored to the client's assets and environment that support and strengthen the client's ability to manage the pragmatic aspects of life." When asked, Barkley affirmed "this is where well-qualified ADHD Coaches can be of maximum benefit to adults with ADHD."[50]

Skills coaching is employed in many fields to help a client, patient, athlete, performer, or student improve his or her performance and competence. It is an important aspect of, but not sufficient unto itself to be, ADHD Coaching. However, without the skills to support sustained change, people with ADHD often find that simple life coaching isn't effective, leading to further discouragement. Therefore development of these skills, and the systems and strategies tailored to the client's resources and environment, is an absolutely necessary part of ADHD Coaching.

EDUCATION

The final element of ADHD Coaching is providing the science and research-based information that helps clients to understand ADHD and how it might be affecting them. Just as understanding the cause of any problem—from diagnosing back pain to car engine trouble—gives one a better foundation from which to solve the problem, simply understanding ADHD and how it manifests, empowers clients to deal more effectively with the challenges that result from having this kind of brain.[51]

Additionally, knowledge helps to de-stigmatize ADHD and the challenges associated with it. To quote the title of the famous book by Kate Kelly and Peggy Ramundo, when clients—and their families—discover that they are not "lazy, stupid, or crazy,"[52] it makes a significant difference in outlook as well as in ability to effectively deal with the challenges predicated by ADHD.[53]

ADHD Coaches also become experts in additional resources that might be of use to clients, and offer these for their client's consideration when warranted. Referrals to doctors, psychotherapists, tutors, nutritionists, professional organizers, educational materials, etc., are a regular part of the educational aspect of ADHD Coaching.

PULLING IT ALL TOGETHER

Twenty years of coaching individuals affected by ADHD and a growing body of research have resulted in an increasingly clear definition of what ADHD Coaching is and what makes it effective.

We know that ADHD Coaching involves education about ADHD, which in itself is liberating, giving the clients a context in which to better understand themselves and their behaviors, reducing the stigma of those behaviors, and opening the door to appropriately targeted treatments and strategies for coping with ADHD.[54]

We know that ADHD Coaching involves the collaborative development of strengths-based systems and strategies that help the client manage the details of life. This is the part of the process referred to as skills coaching that promotes both the conscious awareness of resources and abilities, and the development of conscious competence.

This is the part of the process that produces the scaffolding or prosthetic environment that supports the client when ADHD symptoms manifest.[55]

And we know that ADHD Coaching involves the collaborative, goal-oriented, supportive process called life coaching. This is the part of the process that concentrates on strengthening identity and values, identifying client goals and priorities, and facilitating the sustained change that leads to the achievement of those goals and eventually to optimal life satisfaction.[56]

It is when these three elements are blended, each employed as necessary, that ADHD clients find themselves living well with their ADHD. They find themselves becoming more self-aware, less overwhelmed, more effective, and ultimately, happier and more satisfied with their lives.[57]

ADHD COACH TRAINING PROGRAMS

06

If your goal is to become a professional ADHD Coach, the ACO recommends that you train for either a PAAC certification (see chapter 8), or for one of the recognized life coach certifications (see chapter 7) plus at least 35 hours of ADHD Coach specific training. This chapter can help you figure out which route to go, and which courses to take to fulfill those requirements.

Most programs in this comprehensive list of ADHD Coach training programs are specialty trainings. This means they assume or require that you have previously been, or are concurrently being, trained as a life coach from an accredited life coach training program. A few of the programs listed here are, or include, the life coach training.

Some of these trainings are aimed at professionals from related fields who wish to add ADHD Coaching to their skill set. Some accommodate people who want to learn more about ADHD and how to master it, either for themselves or for a family member. Some are for coaches interested specifically in career coaching or coaching youth. Some are offered in Spanish or Hebrew. One is even offered in Turkish. Most are distance learning programs.

Before you dive into this chapter, decide on your goals. What do you hope to get out of ADHD Coach training? Are you doing this to become an ADHD Coach, to add more depth to your current skill set, or for personal reasons? Do you do well with distance learning? How much time and money can you invest?

Once you know where you want to end up, read through the offerings, which are listed here in alphabetical order, and look for the ones that are the best fit for you. Then, contact the program instructors or administrators to find out when the next class begins and what kind of commitment you'll be making in terms of time and money. Some instructors will allow you to sit in on an introductory class. You may also want to talk with people who've already been through the program to see what they think of it. You can find graduates of these training programs listed among the members of the ACO at ADHDCoaches.org.

And please note the following caveats.

First, in order to clearly distinguish between the Center for Credentialing and Education (CCE) and ICF's Continuing Coach Education (CCE) hours, the latter are referred to here as Continuing Coach Education Units or CCEU. The ICF, because it is the accrediting body for CCEU, and the

CCE, because it endorses the same standard, both accept CCEU as approved coach training hours.

Second, accreditations are listed for each program. You should pay attention to both the accrediting body and level of accreditation, as they represent different degrees and quality of training. CCEU-, ACSTH-, CACEU-, and AACSTH-approved programs are approved on an hour-by-hour basis and may be specialty trainings rather than complete coach training programs. Fully accredited programs that have ICF's ACTP or PAAC's AACTP designations are comprehensive programs that take students through a structured training from basics to preparing students for certification.

Third, every effort has been made to make the following list of ADHD Coach training programs complete and accurate. If you do find errors, omissions, or dead links, please contact the publisher so the mistakes can be corrected in the next edition.

Finally, the content of this chapter has been provided by the trainers themselves with minimal editing, which you might want to keep in mind as you evaluate these programs. Additionally, the mentioning of a school or program here is simply for your information. It is not intended as an endorsement of products or services.

ADD COACH ACADEMY (ADDCA)

This training is for: Anyone interested in deepening their understanding of ADHD and/or becoming an ADHD Coach.

From their website: The ADD Coach Academy is a nationally/internationally recognized coach training program with students participating from the US, Canada, France, Switzerland, Iceland, Israel, Australia, and beyond. We provide innovative, high-quality ADHD Coach training delivered by professional certified coaches. Our instructors use proven core proprietary coaching skills and models honed through many years of training and coaching individuals with ADHD. These proprietary coaching skills and models are the foundation for our "gold standard" ADHD Coach training program. Year after year, the Academy graduates the largest and most respected group of ADHD Coaches in the world.

Course descriptions:

Basic ADHD Coach Training: Learn the fundamental core skills of the coaching process and gain a greater understanding of how the coaching process positively impacts clients with ADHD. The Basic Coach Training Program, part of our AACTP and ACTP Accredited Program, is designed for those students who want to gain a working understanding of the Academy's ADHD proprietary coaching models, and learn how to successfully apply them. This program leads to ADDCA's AAC and AACC credentials.

Advanced ADHD Coach Training: For an individual who wishes to become a professional coach—or just develop exceptional coaching skills—register for the Advanced ADHD Coach Training Program, the most comprehensive and effective training program for new and experienced coaches. The Advanced program includes all of the modules from the Basic program and is part of our AACTP and ACTP Accredited Program. During the Advanced Coach Training Program, each student will focus on learning and practicing the coaching process, skills and models in depth. This program leads to ADDCA's ACG and ACCG credentials.

Professional Advanced ADHD Coach Training Program: The Professional Advanced ADHD Coach Program (PACG) is an advanced level program designed for coaches who have already been trained in core coaching competencies and who want to add the ADHD Coaching component to their skill sets. This program will introduce you to ADDCA's proven, proprietary coaching models and strategies that will add powerful new tools to your current coaching skill set. If you are already confidently coaching your clients using the core ICF competencies, then our Professional

Advanced program will be perfect for you! This program leads to ADDCA's PACG and ACCG credentials.

<u>Mastery ADHD Coach Training (300-Level)</u>: This advanced program will take your coaching skills to a deeper level of mastery and has the added value of being ICF approved for 30 CCEU, which you can use for re-certification. It consists of 5 modules of four sessions each, each 90 minutes long. The training consists of reviewing the steps and tools of the QuestVersation© and practicing integrating the ADDCA models more fully into your coaching. These are practical sessions with feedback and discussion of how and why specific models and strategies were employed in a variety of different coach scenarios. The sessions also focus on practicing the skill sets and models specifically within the context of applying the PAAC coaching competencies to a variety of class scenarios.

General information:
- Webpage: http://www.addca.com
- Email: via webform
- Phone: 800-915-7702
- Founder and President: David Giwerc, MCAC, MCC
- Director of Training: Barbara Luther, MCAC, MCC
- Instructor: Jille Bartolome, MCC
- Instructor: Roger DeWitt, PCC, PACG
- Instructor: Laurie Dupar, PMHNP, RN, PCC

- Instructor: Cameron Gott, PCC, SCAC
- Instructor: Jay Perry, MCC
- Instructor: Elizabeth Vieira-Richard, MCC
- Instructor: Jerry Wistrom, PCC
- Accreditations: ICF ACTP, PAAC AACTP, CCE accredited
- Certifications upon completion: ADDCA Associate Coach (AAC), ADDCA Associate Certified Coach (AACC), ADDCA Coach Graduate (ACG), Professional ADDCA Coach Graduate (PACG), ADDCA Certified Coach Graduate (ACCG)

ADD IN THE SPIRIT COACH TRAINING (ASCT)

This training is for: Anyone interested in becoming an ADHD Coach who wants more than a simple pragmatic approach.

Course description: Madelyn Griffith-Haynie, ADHD Coaching field co-founder and designer/developer of the world's first ADHD-specific coach training curriculum, and Peggy Ramundo, co-author of *You Mean I'm Not Lazy, Stupid or Crazy?!* and *The ADDed Dimension*, offer an ADHD Coach training program that uses a spiritual framework for both coaching and coach training while still addressing the pragmatic aspects of life. Students will become knowledgeable in material drawn from the books *Coaching with Spirit*, *A Course in Miracles*, *How Can I Help?* and more.

General information:

- Webpage: http://addcoaching.com/train_info.php
- Email: coachpeggyramundo@gmail.com
- Phone: 513-288-9821
- Instructor: Madelyn Griffith-Haynie, CTP, CMC, ACT, MCC, SCAC
- Instructor: Peggy Ramundo, ACT, SCAC
- Accreditations: None at this time
- Certification upon completion: ASCT Graduate

ADHD/ASD COACH TRAINING—UNITED KINGDOM

This training is for: People, including parents and professionals, who have previous experience with ADHD.

From their website: Jan Assheton is an experienced Coach and Trainer and can teach you a range of strategies to manage your condition, or can teach you to become a Coach to help others manage their ADHD or Asperger's.

Course description: An 8 week on-line training program requiring the submission of four pieces of written work and a final presentation followed by six months' supervised practice. Certificate only upon satisfactory completion of both course and practicum.

General information:

- Webpage: http://www.janassheton.co.uk
- Email: coaching4adhd@gmail.com
- Phone: +44 1704 879039
- Founder and Instructor: Jan Assheton, BA, RGN, RSCN
- Accreditations: None at this time
- Certification upon completion: Course completion certificate

ADHD COACH TRAINING—ISRAEL

This training is for: Coaches, teachers, school counselors, psychologists, occupational art and music therapists, etc., who have a background working with children and/or adults with ADHD and/or learning disabilities. All participants must have a coaching certificate from an accredited coach training school and must be fluent in Hebrew. This is an in-person training offered by the Bar Ilan University Department of Continuing Education in Israel.

Course descriptions:

ADHD Coach Training: Training coaches in a behavioral coaching model specifically designed for working with ADHD clients of all ages, with a special focus on working with college students, professionals, and teens. The model utilizes NLP techniques, EFT, CBT and mindfulness within the framework of co-active behavioral coaching. Subjects include: goal setting, self-monitoring and emotional regulation, social skills, time management, strategies to enhance motivation and learning. The course is offered by the Bar Ilan University Department of Continuing Education. This in-person ADHD Coach training program is taught in Hebrew.

Coaching ADHD families: Parents and Children: The goal of the course is to provide coaches with the skills to coach parents and children in ADHD families. Participants learn a group coaching model for working with parents and children together, in addition to coaching parents or children separately. The parent coaching model is derived from the Covey model of pro-active parenting. The children's coaching model is based on the adult model and includes teaching self-management skills for routine building, behavior regulation and school success. The course is offered by the Bar Ilan University Department of Continuing Education. This in-person ADHD Coach training program is taught in Hebrew.

General information:
• Webpage: http://lisagrossman.com/
• Email: lisagrossman@012.net.il
• Phone: +972 50-2248220

- Founder and Instructor: Lisa Grossman, MA, MEd, CPCC, SCAC, Licensed Master Coach and Supervisor, ILCC (Israel Coaches Organization)
- Accreditations: Bar Ilan University
- Certification upon completion: Course graduate

AMERICAN COACHING ASSOCIATION (ACA)

This training is for: Anyone interested in deepening their understanding of ADHD and/or becoming an ADHD Coach.

Course description: The ACA provides periodic ADHD Coach training programs at various locations that are delivered in a three-day workshop format. This training is invaluable for the novice who wants to learn about coaching as well as for the experienced coach who wants to broaden or deepen their repertoire of skills. The ACA also provides *Distance Learning with Workbook*. This is a good format for participants who want to move at their own pace.

General information:
- Webpage: http://www.americoach.org
- Email: via webform
- Phone: 610-825-8572
- Founder and Instructor: Sue Sussman, MEd, MCC
- Accreditations: CCE accredited
- Certification upon completion: ACA Graduate

CAREER SERVICES SPECIALTY TRAINING (CSST)

This training is for: Master level and/or seasoned ADHD Coaches, trained from an accredited program.

Course description: This 6-week distance learning class is designed to give accredited, seasoned ADHD Coaches the tools needed to work on the "career piece" with clients. It includes an overview of the career development process; learning about interest clusters and personality factors and how to administer and interpret these assessments, and correlate the results of with potential careers or jobs; and exploring the other pieces of an individual's "puzzle" (values, aptitudes, repeated patterns, focus patterns, and challenges/accommodations), helping clients to gain insights into good career choices. Participants will also learn techniques to help clients with resumes, interviewing, and other job search/retention strategies. Class is followed by one-on-one supervision working with an actual client. Session to be arranged. Graduates of this course earn 13 CCEU.

General information:
- Webpage: https://edgefoundation.org/cceu
- Email: dvonpressentin@edgefoundation.org
- Phone: 206-632-9497
- Program Administrator: Denise Von Pressentin
- Co-Founder and Instructor: Wilma Fellman, MEd, LPC

- Co-Founder and Instructor: Victoria Roche, MSW, PCC
- Accreditations: ICF CCEU
- Certification upon completion: Career Services Specialty (CSS)

COACH APPROACH FOR ORGANIZERS

Coach Approach has two distinct training programs: a foundation coach training program for professional organizer coaches and an advanced training program of individual courses for coaches who have 60 or more hours of coach-specific training and 75 or more client hours. Both training programs teach ADHD Coaching. The coach courses are described below separately under the headings: Foundation Coach Training Program and Advanced Coach Training Program.

Foundation Coach Training Program

This training is for: Experienced and active professional organizers and productivity consultants

From their website: These foundation courses provide a strong, comprehensive groundwork in coaching skills and strategies in the many applications of coaching to the work professional organizers and productivity consultants do. The entire program has earned ICF's Approved Coach-Specific Training Hours (ACSTH) status. Foundation courses must be taken in order, as listed. Graduation from the five-course program can be accomplished in a year (depending on when you begin); there are breaks between courses, ranging in length from two to nine weeks.

Course descriptions:

Coaching Essentials (CE): CE is a stand-alone course designed to train organizers in the use of great, basic coaching skills and strategies designed specifically for organizers for their work with clients. This is intensive, basic coach training, including 18 powerful receptive and active coaching skills and instruction in the best practices and ethics of coaching. Skills competence is developed through trainer feedback and small group support. This course may be all the coach training you'll want for the kind of organizing or productivity work you do—or it may be the start of an entirely new direction for your business. Coaching enables you to create powerful and accountable partnerships with your clients. This course is offered three times a year and is the prerequisite for the following four foundation courses that must be taken in order. Graduates of this course earn 15 CCEU and 18.75 ACSTH.

Strengths-Based Coaching (SBC): Identify and coach to a client's strengths. Learn to work with a client's values and needs to provide self-knowledge and motivate change. We will also use the text: *The Processing Modalities Guide: Identify and Use Specific Strengths for Better Functioning* (Denslow Brown, Hickory Guild Press, 2012) as a lens to individual strengths and sensitivities. Identify your own modality profile and your best learning strategies for creating coaching competence. Collaborate with clients in identifying their modality style and designing organizing systems built on their strengths (insights which will serve them indefinitely). SBC is offered twice a year, in the spring and the fall. Graduates of this course earn 9.5 CCEU and 11.875 ACSTH.

Brain-Based Coaching (BBC): Learn to collaborate with and coach clients who live with the brain-based challenges organizers often encounter in our work: ADHD, depression and anxiety. Coaching strategies are critical for working ethically, openly and successfully with any client with organizing and/or executive functioning challenges. Speak to a client about the impact of their brain-based condition on the organizing and coaching work—and then design a positive relationship and organizing strategy with your client. Coach a client to use support and self-care strategies. Learn when a referral to a mental health professional is required—and how to handle that coaching conversation with compassion and directness. Clarify the ethical issues, your personal and professional boundaries, and explore the possibilities of collaborative work with other professionals. BBC is offered once a year in the fall. Graduates of this course earn 11 CCEU and 13.75 ACSTH.

Life and ADHD Coaching (LAC): The training in stand-alone coaching provides you a powerful complement to organizing work. Learn the 17 additional receptive and active coaching skills which are specifically useful in working with people with a variety of organizing and executive functioning challenges, whether they have ADHD or not. Support a client in moving toward "A Life that Fits" their passions, values and needs. Training includes the core skills, best practices and ethics of ADHD Coaching, including our Essential Structures (ADHD Education, Self-Knowledge, Action and Support), self- talk, boundaries, etc. LAC is offered once a year in winter. Graduates of this course earn 11 CCEU and 13.75 ACSTH.

Organizer Coach Integration (OCI): The last foundation course provides structure for an integration of the multifaceted coaching methodologies which complement organizing work. Students clarify the definition of coaching within their own organizing work and design individualized coaching practices to solidify coaching competence. Graduates of this course earn 8 CCEU and 10 ACSTH.

Coaching Skills Lab (CSL) (Elective Foundation Training): This supplemental training is for those who have completed the *Coaching Essentials* course, so that they can continue to work with a trainer to practice coaching skills and build coaching experience and confidence. In each class, one coaching session takes place with a student coach and client. Other participants serve as active observers as does the trainer. The trainer or coach pauses the coaching session one or more times during the coaching. At these pauses, the trainer will realign the coaching—or ask each observer to offer a point of curiosity, powerful question, or possible direction. Graduates of this course earn 6 CCEU and 7.5 ACSTH.

Advanced Coach Training Program

This training is for: Advanced training and continuing education credits for ADHD Coaches and Organizer Coaches. All students must have at minimum 60 coach-specific training hours and 75 client hours (unless otherwise specified).

From their website: Our advanced training program was designed by experienced trainers who are credentialed coaches with both strong ADHD and 'vanilla' coach training. Although ADHD is not in the title of every course, the training content consistently addresses the needs of ADHD clients (unless otherwise specified).

Course descriptions:

ADHD Education: Knowledge is Power (AE): Clients with ADHD ADD-like symptoms benefit from an ongoing discovery process about their brain's capacity and how to make the most of it. Engage your clients' curiosity and commitment to self-knowledge in service to an enjoyable, accomplished and accountable life. This course models how to clearly and concisely share ADD essentials. Trainers: Ari Tuckman, PsyD and Denslow Brown, MCC. Graduates of this course earn 7.5 CCEU.

Coaching the ADHD Client from Awareness to Action (CAC): This is graduate-level, advanced training in ADHD Coaching techniques. You will be trained in the use of Cameron Gott's AEC Coaching Model (Awareness-Engagement-Completion). This is a method to work with clients in a growth-change process, supporting their integration of two life-changing training concepts: Articulating Curiosity and Curious Accountability. Distinctions are made for Hyperactive and Inattentive subtypes. The course includes coaching demonstrations, case studies, and weekly 2-person skills building partnerships. Trainer: Cameron Gott, PCC. Graduates of this course earn 10.5 CCEU and 13.125 ACSTH.

Core Competency Intensives (CCI): Offered 1 – 4 times a year, each 5-session course focuses on a critical broad area of coaching competence referencing the ICF and PAAC lists. Registration is limited to no more than seven students to facilitate the seminar/instruction/lab format and meet group mentor coaching requirements. Graduates of this course earn 7.5 CCEU and 9.375 ACSTH.

Graduate (and ADHD Coach) Book Analysis (GBA): Offered periodically, the six- session GBA courses use an assigned text (usually a coaching and/or ADHD text) and a facilitated discussion format. Specific pages are assigned for each teleclass. The two GBA courses for 2014 will use the texts: *Body-Centered Coaching* by Marlena Field (mind-body connection strategies to increase awareness, intuition, courage and action) and *Lean-in* by Sheryl Sandberg (women's internal challenges to expressing leadership and values and the workplace and family issues confronting men and women). Register for Option 2 to add skills-building partner work and 30 minutes additional class time each week for coaching demo and discussions. Graduates of option 1 of this course earn 6 CCEU and 7.5 ACSTH. Graduates of option 2 earn 9 CCEU and 11.25 ACSTH.

Holistic Time Coaching (HTC): This 7-week course trains students in strategies for coaching clients into a time management system that fits their life and ways of being. We will be using as our guide the *True for You Time Management Workbook* (included) by Julie Gray, Holistic

Time Coach, and will walk you through each phase of the holistic time management process. The training in this new methodology is experiential: students will explore their own time use approaches and coach each other into new insights and actions. Trainers: Julie Gray, ACC, COC and Denslow Brown, MCC. Graduates of this course earn 10.5 CCEU.

Leadership Coaching I: Coaching the Leader (LC I): This course works with a number of concepts that the leadership coach needs to master (as a coach and as a leader) to best serve this client population. We will study various leadership models (distinguishing Essence Leading and Ego Leading) and explore critical concepts such as cultivating and articulating vision, motivation, the leader in relationship, and change management. Trainers for both leadership courses: Ellen Faye, CPO, COC and Cameron Gott, PCC. Graduates of this course earn 9 CCEU.

Leadership Coaching II: Group Dynamics (LC II): The second leadership course explores coaching the leader in relationship to the group through communication, collaboration and team building techniques which support clients in leading effective, productive and healthy teams. Selected leadership measurement tools will be evaluated for client use. The last two classes focus on how to develop and lead experiential team meetings and workshops. Graduates of this course earn 9 CCEU.

Life Direction Coaching (LDC): By force or by choice more people than ever have to reinvent their careers—and their lives. This training will uniquely equip you to handle the urgency for those that need to forge a new career path or life direction. Learn to use the proven tools and coaching strategies, created and taught by Laura Berman Fortgang, MCC and based on her book *Now What? 90 Days to a New Life Direction.* Her 12-week, Life-Blueprint® coaching model takes a client from confused to focused and on-track. Graduates of this course earn 15 CCEU.

Productivity Coaching: Fostering Awareness, Perspective & Action (PC): Coaching strategies to address client productivity challenges are the focus of this 6-session course. While the course's coaching principles and insights apply to any productivity client work, we will use the versatile and explicit Productivity Chain model developed by Casey Moore, The Productivity Coach, in her book *Stop Organizing Start Producing.* A copy of the book and completion of the Productivity Chain Self-Assessment are included with registration. Students will also meet in weekly 2-person skills work and students develop a productivity client case study during the training period. Trainers: Casey Moore, COC, CPO and Denslow Brown, MCC. Graduates of this course earn 9 CCEU.

Group Mentor Coaching (GMC): Developed to strengthen coaching competence, this course includes instruction as well as coaching sessions. In each class, one coaching session will take place with a coach and client from the student group. The coaching will be interrupted at key points to discuss the coaching dynamic, flow and powerful directions. Participants will contribute feedback and alternative choices during the breaks and debriefing. ICF and PAAC Core competencies will be identified. Registration is limited to five to seven students to facilitate the seminar/instruction/lab format and meet group mentor coaching requirements. Graduates of this course earn 7.5 CCEU and 9.375 ACSTH.

On-Track / Back On-Track with Your Coaching Business (OT/BOT): Are you confident of your path to success with the coaching part of your business? Maybe you're looking for the transition ramp from organizer (with coaching skills) to a standalone coaching business? In this unique new course, we'll work to get you *on-track* or *back on-track*. You'll get clear about the roadblocks and create alternate routes to get past them. Your partner coach and the down-the-road second class meeting will help you direct your coaching business to success. Trainer: Andrea Sharb, COC, ACC, CPO-CD, CPO. Graduates of this course earn 3 Professional Development CCEU.

Client Enrollment: Best Practices for Organizer Coaches (CE/BP): How successful are you at enrolling clients? Do you land the prospect every time, only to discover you're not a good match? Is your enrollment process so thorough that you scare prospects off? We'll distinguish enrolling organizing vs. coaching clients, identify the different stages of enrollment, and improve communication accordingly. Participants will gain clarity and create a manageable set of best practices for the enrolling process. What would consistently signing up well-qualified coaching clients do for you? While accountability partnerships are not course requirements, you are welcome to reach out to other students to set up this support for yourself. Also open to foundation students. Trainer: Andrea Sharb, COC, ACC, CPO-CD, CPO. Graduates of this course earn 3 Professional Development CCEU.

General information:

- Webpage: http://www.coachapproachfororganizers.com
- Email: denslow@coachapproachfororganizers.com
- Phone: 417-683-1064
- Founder and Director of Training: Denslow Brown, CPO, CPO-CD, SCAC, MCC
- Curriculum Co-Designer and Senior Trainer: Cameron Gott, PCC, SCAC

- Partner Training Program: Now What? with Laura Berman Fortgang, MCC
- Trainer: Andrea Sharb, ACC, CPO-CD, COC
- Trainer: Ari Tuckman, PsyD, MBA
- Assistant Trainer: Yvonne Trostli, COC
- Assistant Trainer: Julie Gray, ACC, COC
- Assistant Trainer: Casey Moore, CPO, COC
- Assistant Trainer: Ellen Faye, CPO, COC
- Accreditations: ICF ACSTH status has been granted for the entire foundation training program and much of the advanced training. ICF ACTP and PAAC AACTP pending.
- Certifications upon completion: Certified Organizer Coach (COC), Certified ADHD Organizer Coach (CAOC), Certified Organizer Life Coach (COLC), Certified Productivity Leadership Coach (CPLC).

COACHING CHILDREN & TEENS WITH ADHD AT UNH

This is an in-person training comprised of six one-day workshops conducted at either the Portsmouth or Manchester campuses of the University of New Hampshire.

This training is for: A broad range of professionals, including special educators, teachers, mental health professionals, guidance and pastoral counselors, healthcare providers and other professionals who work with children and teens with ADHD.

Course description: ADHD begins in early childhood and can last through the teen years into adulthood. Children with ADHD may have difficulty focusing, listening, sitting still, following instructions, and keeping emotions in check. Increasingly, research is showing that coaching can be a powerful tool in helping children and teens deal with the difficulties they face as a result of ADHD. Coaches can help children and teens with ADHD learn how to manage their time, break down daunting tasks into manageable steps, keep themselves organized, think proactively, use mindfulness techniques, and learn to check their thinking/acting at intervals. This Certificate Program is composed of six required one-day workshops. Three provide a basic foundation for coaching children and teens and the other three focus specifically on coaching children and teens with ADHD. This certificate program is offered at Pease in Portsmouth and in Manchester New Hampshire.

General information:
- Webpage: https://learn.unh.edu/training/certificate
- Email: anitaremig@gmail.com
- Phone: 603-781-3892
- Founder and Instructor: Dr. Anita Remig
- Accreditations: University of New Hampshire
- Certification upon completion: UNH Coaching Children & Teens with ADHD Certificate

COACHING TDA—SPAIN & SOUTH AMERICA

This training is for: Fluent Spanish speakers who wish to specialize in coaching people affected by ADHD. Participants must have had at least 60 hours of formal life coaching training or currently be enrolled in an ICF Accredited Coach Training Program.

Course description: This Spanish language ADHD Coach specialty training, pioneered in Spain and Latin America, offers the latest scientific information to help participants better understand how ADHD affects people. As specialty life coaches, we need to know and understand the strengths and challenges that occur in the lives our clients with ADHD so that we may effectively coach them. Graduates of this course earn 17.5 CCEU.

General information:
- Webpage: http://olacoach.com/cursos/coaching-tda-h
- Email: lupitav@lupitavolio.com
- Phone: +34 61 623 54 52
- Founder and Instructor: Lupita Volio, MCC, SCAC
- Accreditations: ICF CCEU
- Certifications upon completion: Course Graduate

FASTTRACK COACH ACADEMY

This training is for: Individuals who want to become certified coaches (new coaches will acquire all the training and mentor coaching hours needed to apply for ICF's ACC Credential), already-certified coaches who want to use their FastTrack hours for re-certification or toward their new higher-level PCC/MCC certification requirements, and business leaders who want to add professional coaching skills to their leadership skills toolbox.

Course description: This is an ICF ACC-compliant life coach training program. It is often taken in conjunction with the JST Coaching program in order to specialize in coaching youth affected by ADHD, or in conjunction with the American Coaching Association ADHD Coach training program in order to specialize in coaching adults affected by ADHD.

General information:
- Webpage: http://fasttrackcoachacademy.com
- Email: coach@fasttrackcoachacademy.com
- Phone: 610-825-8572
- Founder and Instructor: Sue Sussman, MEd, MCC
- Accreditations: ICF ACSTH, ACTP pending
- Certification upon completion: FastTrack Coach Academy Graduate

FRAMING THE ADHD EXPERIENCE BEFORE ONE-ON-ONE COACHING BEGINS

This training is for: Experienced ADHD Coaches who wish to learn how to use this proven foundational program to help clients lay the groundwork for even greater success.

Course description: When working with ADHD clients, is very important to first educate them on the cognitive, emotional and behavioral effects of their ADHD, which helps set them up for even greater success during coaching. The first peer-reviewed study ever published on the efficacy of ADHD Coaching[58] was based on outcomes from the approach taught in this program. This distance learning course teaches coaches how to create a solid framework with their ADHD clients, strengthening the client-coach relationship before coaching even begins. Included are the strategies used in the study, Plan For Success, and a copy of the Kubik Outcome Rating Scale (KORS), an instrument used in this program at no additional cost (guide is included). Graduates of this course earn 12 CCEU.

General information:
- Webpage: http://bridgetosuccess.net
- Email: joyce@bridgetosuccess.net
- Phone: 440-933-8309
- Founder and Instructor: Joyce Kubik, BA, CMC

- Accreditations: ICF CCEU
- Certifications upon completion: Course Graduate

IMPACT COACHING ACADEMY (ICA)

This training is for: Anyone interested in deepening their understanding of ADHD and becoming an ADHD Coach. Coaches who complete the training can specialize in working only with ADHD clients, or utilize the training to work more effectively with any of their clients who have ADHD.

Course descriptions:

ICA Professional Life Coach Training: The Professional Life Coach (CPC) Training program is for new coaches, who will learn professional ethical guidelines, and coaching skills and competencies. The Master Professional Coach (MPC) training program is for experienced coaches who want additional training to achieve mastery of the professional coaching competencies and skills. Both programs are 30 hours in duration and are available in a live teleclass format over nine weeks, or a live in-person intensive during a three day weekend training. Professionals who do not require course certification may take the self-paced study format of the Professional Life Coach Training program.

ICA ADHD Coach Training: The ICA-Certified ADHD Coach (CAC) program provides a comprehensive understanding of how ADHD works and how to effectively coach clients with ADD/ADHD. Participants will learn about the nuts and bolts of ADHD, how limiting beliefs get in the way, and the importance of a strong personal foundation. Every module has coaching tools participants can add to their tool box, complete with detailed instructions on how and when to use the tools. This program will prepare participants to coach ADHD clients in all key areas of life and help them deal with distraction, disorganization, and lack of focus. The training also includes important business building tools, including how to market and enroll clients, as well as the basics of how to organize and run their coaching business.

The ICA-Certified Master ADHD Coach (CMAC) is an advanced level of training for ICA-Certified ADHD Coaches, and focuses on specific challenges in marriage, parenting, career, and more. It provides the coach who wishes to specialize in the field of ADHD with the advanced knowledge, tools, and skill set required to work effectively with ADHD clients.

Both courses are 30 hours in duration and are available in a live teleclass format over 10 weeks, or a live in-person intensive during a three day weekend training.

General information:

• Webpage: http://www.impactcoachingacademy.com

- Email: tereasa@impactcoachingacademy.com
- Phone: 800-686-1463
- Founder and CEO: Frankie Doiron, BCC, MCRC
- ADHD Program Instructor: Tereasa Jones, MS, SCAC, MCRC
- Accreditations: ICF CCEU and ACSTH pending
- Certifications upon completion: ICA-Certified ADHD Coach (CAC) and ICA-Certified Master ADHD Coach (CMAC)

JST COACHING

This training is for: New coaches interested in exploring ADHD youth coaching and trained coaches and allied professionals who wish to coach ADHD youth. Courses are offered in Spanish and Turkish as well as English.

Course descriptions:

Coaching Teens & College Students with ADHD: This course is the first to focus on coaching teens and college students with ADHD. General teen/college life coaching will be covered in this course and will follow the ICF core competencies. This is an informative AND interactive training program designed to provide coaching strategies, hands-on practice and business building ideas to get you started with your new client base with confidence and expertise. All of the programs may be completed as a 15-week distance learning program or a 3-day intensive training option. Graduates of this course earn 30 CCEU and 22 ACSTH.

Advanced Coaching Skills Practicum: The Advanced Coaching Skills Practicum teleclass is designed help experienced coaches fine-tune their coaching skills in a small group setting while earning CCEU. A minimum of six months of coaching youth required for admission to this class. The course will focus on role-playing with feedback from the facilitator and peer coaches and will focus on ADHD Coaching and life coaching core competencies. Graduates of this course earn 8 CCEU.

Coaching Children with ADHD: This teleclass focuses on how to shift the coaching process for success with children ages 8 – 12, how to include parents into the coaching process, and provides tools for accountability and rewards for children and families as well as handouts for use with students in the classroom and at home. Graduates of this course earn 7.5 CCEU.

General information:
- Webpage: http://www.jstcoach.com
- Email: info@jstcoach.com
- Phone: 703-548-3161

- Founder and President: Jodi Sleeper-Triplett, MCC, SCAC, BCC
- Instructor: Russell Colver CPCC, SCAC, BCC
- Instructor: Christina Fabrey, BCC, ACAC
- Instructor: Elgiz Henden, CLC, PCC
- Instructor: Kimber Nelson, CPC
- Instructor: JoAnn Skinner, ACAC, ACC, BCC
- Instructor: Loretta Spindel, JD, PCC, BCC
- Instructor: Harriet Steinberg, RN, MN, PCC, SCAC, BCC
- Instructor: Dulce Torres, LPC-S, BCC
- Accreditations: ICF CCEU, ICF ACTP pending, CCE accredited
- Certification upon completion: JST Graduate

LIVE ADHD FREE

This training is for: Both for professionals who have ADHD or who have grown up living in a family with ADHD and wish to learn more about living ADHD free, and for trained life coaches who want to specialize in coaching people affected by ADHD.

Course descriptions: A 16 week distance-learning program specializing in teaching ICF Coaching Competencies, offering hands-on coaching experiences with clients, weekly one-on-one coaching practice with instructor, and

a one-of-a-kind-model for personal ADHD transformation:
the VIP (Values-Identity-Purpose Model for sourcing our
inner wisdom). Because our students coach real clients
throughout the program, by the time they graduate they
have already begun to build their practices. They continue
to do so after graduation using the marketing tools they
learn in the program. Students are accepted into the
program based on an application, an understanding of the
ADHD brain, previous experience and education, and a
sincere motivation to work with the ADHD population.

General Information:
• Webpage: http://liveadhdfree.com
• Email: carol@liveadhdfree.com
• Phone: 617-524-7670
• Founder and Instructor: Carol Gignoux, MEd, ICF-CFI,
  SCAC, CUCG
• Accreditations: ICF CCEU pending
• Certifications upon completion: Live ADHD Free Graduate
  Certificate

MENTORCOACH

This training is for: Anyone interested in becoming a
coach. MentorCoach has historically provided coach
training for individuals in the helping professions. Alan

Graham, PhD, PCC, MCAC is the Dean of the ADHD Coach Training Program within MentorCoach.

From their website: MentorCoach® is the leading coach training school based on the integration of evidence-based coaching and the new science of Positive Psychology. Our ICF accredited program blends practice and leading theoretical insights that empower you in the transition toward becoming a masterful coach. The MentorCoach ADHD Coaching Master Classes have been created to give participants the 38 hours of ADHD Coach training that is the minimum required to be credentialed as an Certified ADHD Coach Practitioner (CACP) the first level of ADHD Coach certification through PAAC. The master classes are designed to address the core competencies developed by PAAC.

Course descriptions:

The Positive Psychology and ADHD Coaching Master Class: This curriculum offers much of the nuts and bolts ADHD information needed to be an effective ADHD Coach, such as symptoms/diagnostic methods/medications and, most importantly, viewing each client as an entire individual. An expected outcome of this class is for each participant to have their own personal toolbox of interventions that they can use with clients with ADHD. Graduates of this course earn 12 CCEU.

The Positive Psychology and Advanced ADHD Coaching Master Class—Adults: This course curriculum is designed to put the coach's skill set into action with clients. Each week is dedicated to a specific 'type' of client issue. The class focuses on adults with ADHD-type symptoms as well as issues that are unique to adults with ADHD. Situations related to working with spouses of individuals with ADHD are also addressed. Each participant has an opportunity to present a coaching conversation to the class, with a class debriefing afterwards. Graduates of this course earn 13 CCEU.

The Positive Psychology and Advanced ADHD Coaching Master Class—College Students, Teens, Children and Parents: This course curriculum is designed to put the coach's skill-set into action with clients. Each week is dedicated to a specific 'type' of client. The class focuses on children, teens and young adults with ADHD-type symptoms. Situations related to working with parents of individuals with ADHD are also addressed. Each participant has an opportunity to present a coaching conversation to the class, with a class debriefing afterwards. Graduates of this course earn 13 CCEU.

General information:
- Webpage: http://mentorcoach.com
- Email: info@mentorcoach.com

- Phone: 301-986-5688
- Founder and CEO: Ben Dean PhD, MCC
- Instructor and Dean of the ADHD Program: Alan R. Graham, PhD, MCAC, PCC, SCAC
- Accreditations: ICF ACTP, CCE accredited, PAAC AACTP
- Certification upon completion: Certified MentorCoach (CMC)

LIFE COACH CERTIFICATION

07

A number of life coaching schools certify their graduates, but it should be remembered that such certifications are not industry standards. Based on credentials that ACO members hold, there are three independent life coach certification bodies relevant to ADHD Coaching. They are the International Coach Federation, the International Association of Coaching, and the Center for Credentialing and Education. The following gives you an overview of these three life coach certification options.

INTERNATIONAL COACH FEDERATION (ICF)

The International Coach Federation (ICF), founded in 1995, is the oldest, largest, and most recognized of the life coach certification and accreditation bodies. The ICF's core purpose is to advance the art, science, and practice of professional coaching. As of March 2014, there are over 24,000 members in 114 countries, and the ICF has certified over 11,000 coaches, including 6901 Associate Certified Coaches, 3934 Professional Certified Coaches, and 668 Master Certified Coaches.[59]

THE OPTIONS AND REQUIREMENTS FOR BECOMING AN ICF-CERTIFIED COACH

A number of ADHD Coach training programs, listed in the training section below, have met the standard for ICF Continuing Coach Education (CCE), Accredited Coach Specialty Training Hours (ACSTH), and / or Accredited Coach Training Program (ACTP). The ICF has three levels of certification: Associate Certified Coach (ACC), Professional Certified Coach (PCC), and the Master Certified Coach (MCC). For the ACC and PCC, it also has two paths to certification: either training through an Accredited Coach Training Program (ACTP), or through a portfolio route. The portfolio route is chosen by people who are trained, experienced coaches but who did not graduate from an ICF-accredited coach training school, and is the route taken by many ICF-certified ADHD Coaches. For the MCC certification, there is only the portfolio route.

To give you a feel for the requirements for each level of certification, here are the basics:

• The ACC requires at least 60 hours of coach-specific training and at least 100 hours of client coaching experience. Fees ranges from $100 to $500 USD.

- The PCC requires at least 125 hours of coach-specific training and at least 750 hours of client coaching experience. Fees ranges from $300 to $775 USD.

- The MCC requires at least 200 hours of coach-specific training and at least 2500 hours of client coaching experience. Fees range from $575 to $775.

Applications and additional information for each certification can be found on the ICF website. They can also be found at: http://tinyurl.com/ICFCredentialRequirements2014.

For all three certification levels, in order to retain the credential, ICF certified coaches must obtain a minimum number of hours of continuing education. Renewal applications must be filed every three years.

Website: http://www.coachfederation.org

APPROVED ICF TRAINING PROVIDERS

ICF-approved ADHD Coach training programs are:

- ADD Coach Academy—ACTP
- Coach Approach for Organizers—CCEU and ACSTH, ACTP pending
- Coaching TDA—CCEU
- FastTrack Coach Academy—CCEU and ACSTH, ACTP pending

- Framing the ADHD Experience—CCEU
- JST Coaching—CCEU, ACTP pending
- MentorCoach—ACTP

INTERNATIONAL ASSOCIATION OF COACHING (IAC)

The International Association of Coaching (IAC) is the second life coach certification body founded by Thomas Leonard. His untimely death in February of 2003 delayed the effective launch of this certification for several years as legalities were worked out. As of March 2014, the website lists 1000 members and 54 certified coaches. Aside from the significant differences in age and size of the organization, the important difference in this certification compared to ICF's is that there are no requirements for where or how coaches obtain their knowledge and skill, only that they demonstrate they have it. Here is the description of their certification process.

THE OPTIONS AND REQUIREMENTS FOR BECOMING AN IAC-CERTIFIED COACH

There are two levels of certification: The Certified Masteries Coach (CMC) and the Master Masteries Coach (MMC). The following is the process for becoming certified, downloaded on March 15, 2014.

- Learn and Integrate the IAC Coaching Masteries™ into your life and practice

- Be sure your membership is current

- Try the Part One sample test (free)

- Pay $97 USD for the online exam

- Take and pass the online exam

- Review requirements for the oral exam

- Prepare for the oral exam by recording as many coaching sessions as necessary until you are demonstrating fully the nine Coaching Masteries®

- Pay the $500 USD certification submission fee, and submit two recorded coaching sessions, with two different clients, for evaluation (please thoroughly review the guidelines first). A score sheet with certifiers' comments will be mailed within 6-8 weeks of submitting recordings. In some instances, applicants may be invited to an interview with the certifiers to address questions about specific Masteries. In these cases, the score sheet and certification decision will be provided following completion of this interview

- If you are not already an IAC Masteries Practitioner, or have not previously submitted your first IAC Learning

Agreement: 12 months from your certification date, develop your first personalized Learning Agreement. Pay the $150 USD fee, and submit your Learning Agreement Proposal and schedule a review with a certifier. Continue submitting annual personalized Learning Agreements and maintain your annual membership fee to keep your MMC, CMC, or Masteries Practitioner status current.

Because IAC does not consider the source of your coach training as part of its certification process, you can train for this certification simply by learning the IAC Coaching Masteries™ and integrating them into your practice.

Website: http://www.certifiedcoach.org

CENTER FOR CREDENTIALING AND EDUCATION (CCE)

The Center for Credentialing and Education (CCE) in collaboration with Pat Williams, founder of the Institute for Life Coach Training (ILCT), created the Board Certified Coach credential (BCC) in 2011. This certification is aimed at pre-trained professionals who have advanced degrees and experience equivalent to a majority of the coaching and coach training hours required by ICF to become a certified coach.

Application requirements for becoming a certified coach with the CCE differ based on an applicant's previous training. To obtain a BCC credential, applicants are first required to obtain coach-specific training to cover the educational gap related to the differences (or "gap") between life coaching competencies and their previous training.

Website: http://www.cce-global.org

THE OPTIONS AND REQUIREMENTS FOR BECOMING A CCE-CERTIFIED COACH

You can view the training requirements—which, as mentioned above, vary depending on your previous training and professional background—and download the BCC Exam Candidate Handbook and the BCC Application from their website: http://www.cceglobal.org/BCC

APPROVED CCE TRAINING PROVIDERS

ADHD Coach training programs that are approved BCC training providers are:

- ADD Coach Academy (ADDCA)
- American Coaching Association (ACA)
- JST Coaching
- MentorCoach

ADHD COACH CERTIFICATION

08

PROFESSIONAL ASSOCIATION OF ADHD COACHES (PAAC)

The Professional Association of ADHD Coaches (PAAC) was founded in 2009 by Barbara Luther and Chana Klein to "establish high standards of excellence in our ADHD certification and accreditation programs. We advocate for coaches and the profession of ADHD Coaching, for the benefit of all individuals in need."[60] It became a 501c3 nonprofit in 2010 and began credentialing coaches in 2012.

This certification is closely aligned with and modeled after the ICF certification, but specifically tailored and refined for ADHD Coaches. Unlike life coaching, where there are a number of independently operated certifying organizations, PAAC is the sole organization offering an independent ADHD Coach specialty certification.

THE OPTIONS AND REQUIREMENTS FOR BECOMING A PAAC-CERTIFIED COACH

PAAC offers three levels of certification, which roughly correlate to the three levels of certification offered by the ICF. They are:

• Certified ADHD Coach Practitioner (CACP)

• Professional Certified ADHD Coach (PCAC)

• Master Certified ADHD Coach (MCAC)

Like the ICF, for the CACP and PCAC there are two paths to certification: either training through a PAAC-approved program, or through a portfolio route. For the MCAC, there is only one route.

Each level requires a specific number of coach-specific training hours, ADHD-specific training hours, and mentoring hours. To give you a feel for the requirements for each level of certification, these are the basics:

• The CACP requires 75 coach-specific training hours, 20 ADHD-specific training hours, 20 mentoring hours, and at least 150 hours of client coaching experience. Fee is $200 USD.

• The PCAC requires 150 coach-specific training hours, 40 ADHD-specific training hours, 40 mentoring hours, and at least 600 hours of client coaching experience. Fee is $300 USD.

• The MCAC requires 300 coach-specific training hours, 80 ADHD-specific training hours, 50 mentoring hours, and at least 2000 hours of client coaching experience. Fee is $350.

Website: http://www.paaccoaches.org

APPROVED PAAC TRAINING PROVIDERS

ADHD Coach training programs that are approved PAAC training providers (AACTP programs) are:

• ADD Coach Academy (ADDCA)
• Coach Approach for Organizers (pending)
• MentorCoach

PAAC is accepting applications for AACSTH and CACEU and will soon offer a list of approved programs on the web.

LIABILITY INSURANCE

09

Historically, the life coaching profession has had very little problem with liability. However, if you will be working in corporate, clinical, or educational settings, liability insurance may be required. Alternatively, if you are an independent business person, you may not need liability insurance until you reaches a certain number of clients, or you may not need it at all.

Laws regarding liability insurance vary from place to place, and you will need to explore what is required where you live and work. No matter what your situation, you will want to talk with your legal, financial, and insurance professionals to determine your best course of action.

If you do decide to seek liability insurance, the following are some options to consider.

First, if you have other professional designation(s) for which you carry liability insurance, that insurance may also cover your coaching. Therefore, you should look into that option first.

Second, if you are not already covered, you have choices. You can either become a member of a large professional association and take advantage of the discounted liability insurance rates those organizations offer (as well as their other membership benefits), or go directly to an appropriate insurance carrier.

To help you with those second alternatives, listed in this chapter are the most common options for liability insurance cited by ACO members. Most of these options cover US citizens only. The ICF and CCE options cover citizens of Canada and the UK as well. Citizens of other countries are encouraged to speak with your local experts to determine your best course of action.

In researching rates for this chapter, the insurance carriers were asked to provide a quote for a self-employed life coach with five years' experience working with clients over the phone for 20 hours per week. Your rates may vary depending on the parameters of your coaching business.

Because you must be a member of the professional associations to get a quote for coverage, it was not possible to get insurance quotes from the association's insurance providers. Instead, the current annual membership fees for the professional association are cited along with the insurance carrier's association-specific webpage.

LIABILITY INSURANCE THROUGH PROFESSIONAL ASSOCIATIONS

International Coach Federation (ICF)

Website: http://coachfederation.org

Annual Membership Fee: $245 USD

Insurance Website: http://insurance-icf.com

International Association of Coaching (IAC)

Website: http://www.certifiedcoach.org/

Annual Membership Fee: $149 USD

Insurance Website: http://www.iac.lockton-ins.com/assoc/iac/pl

Center for Credentialing and Education (CCE)

This option is only available to holders of CCE's Board Certified Coach credential.

Website: http://cce-global.org

Annual Membership Fee: $40 USD

Insurance Website: http://insurance-cce-global.com/

American Counseling Association

Website: http://counseling.org/

Annual Membership Fee: $94 or $165 depending on education and experience.

Insurance Website: http://www.hpso.com/

LIABILITY INSURANCE DIRECTLY FROM INSURERS

The Van Wagner Insurance Group
Website: http://www.vanwagnergroup.com/
Rate: $25 USD for $1 million per occurrence and $3 million aggregate limit/year.

Lockton Professional Liability Insurance
Website: http://professionalliabilityinsurance.info
Rate: $124 USD for $1 million per occurrence and $2 million aggregate limit/year.
Comment: Life Coaches are covered under "Counselors and Therapists"

Philadelphia Insurance Companies
Website: https://www.phly.com/productsfw/FWI_LifeCoachIndiv.aspx
Rate: $246 USD for $1 million per occurrence and $3 million aggregate limit/year.

Healthcare Providers Service Organization
Website: http://www.hpso.com/
Rate: $125 USD for $1 million per occurrence and $5 million aggregate limit/year.
Comment: Life Coaches are covered under "Counseling Professionals." This quoted rate includes a $2 USD HPSO membership fee.

10 THE 2013 ACO MEMBERSHIP SURVEY

In early 2013, having experienced steady growth since its founding in 2005, the ACO conducted a membership survey to find out more about its members and, by extension, the entire ADHD Coaching profession.

Some of the questions in the membership survey were designed to collect basic demographic information. Others were to get some idea of how coaches come to the profession, where they get their training, how they work, and more.

About half of membership responded to the survey, with a slightly higher proportion of professional members responding than associate members. Note that the answers provided yield a snapshot of the makeup of the profession as it was then. In the year since the survey was taken, the ACO has grown an additional 20%. If the survey were to be taken today, the results might be somewhat different. With that caveat, the following is a summary of what was learned.

What became clear is that, although ADHD Coaches are a diverse group, there are definite trends. The members are largely women (83%), have ADHD in their family (90%), have a bachelor's degree (90%) or higher (56%), and are at least 50 years of age (72%). Most became coaches because of their life experiences (59%), and have a background either in the medical/helping professions (33%) or education (18%). Most have been coaches from 1 – 4 years (40%), but there are a significant number of more experienced coaches as well: 26% have been coaches for 5 – 10 years and 21% have been coaches for more than 10. Only 13% have been coaching for less than a year. Most work part time (57%) and most are self-employed (87%).

Although this was not part of the survey, over the years coaches have reported working part time for a number of reasons. These include that they are still in training, fitting in a job around family, semi-retired and coaching as a late-life career, or they also have a full time job because they need the income and/or health insurance. Part timers may have only one or two clients.

The reported annual income numbers (in USD) reflect the fact that the profession skews toward part time work and coaches with less than 5 years of experience. 34% make less than $10k per year, 30% make $10k – $35k per year, 18% make $35k – $60k, 9% make $60k-$85k per year, and another 9% make over $85k per year.

In terms of training, 40% report training at ADDCA, 40% at JST Coaching, 14% at FastTrack Academy, 9% at

MentorCoach, 8% at the Optimal Functioning Institute, and 40% in other programs. Most ADHD Coaches participate in multiple training programs over the course of their education and careers.

Regarding certification, 57% of ACO members were certified through at least one of the recognized life or ADHD Coach certifying organizations (CCE, IAC, IAAC, ICF, or PAAC), and another 11% had a certification from one of those organizations pending.

Within the realm of those affected by ADHD, members reported working with diverse and multiple populations:

Men	27%
Women	36%
Couples	20%
Parents	34%
Children/Middle School	20%
Teens/High School	45%
Young Adults/College Students	69%
Adults	80%
Entrepreneurs/Business coaching	39%
Career Coaching	18%
Education Support	27%
Justice System	4%
Other	19%

ADHD Coaches also work in diverse and multiple settings. Most (79%) work one-on-one. An overlapping 39% also or exclusively do group coaching. 77% work via telephone, 56% work via video chat, 50% work in person in their own office, 15% work in person in a school setting, and 11% work in person in a business setting.

The majority of ACO members live in the US (80%), 10% are in Canada, and 10% are in Europe or Australia. Most of the Canadian coaches live in Ontario. Within the US, most ACO members live in states on the East or West Coasts, or around the Great Lakes. With a few exceptions (notably Texas), ADHD Coaches are under-represented in many of the southern, central, and mountain states.

The following graph shows the growth of the ACO since its incorporation.

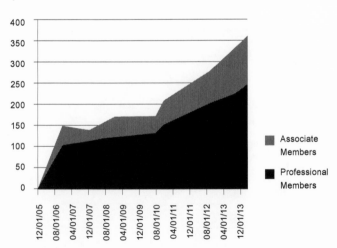

LOOKING
FORWARD

11

Twenty years have brought ADHD Coaching from birth, through youthful growing pains, to the verge of maturity.

Where once there were just a few people working from experience and instinct to help people affected by ADHD understand and master that part of themselves while using their strengths to build a life they love, there are now hundreds (and perhaps thousands) of ADHD Coaches in practice all around the world.

Where once there was no clear definition of what ADHD Coaching is, and no research on its efficacy, there is now a broad consensus as to what comprises ADHD Coaching, and a body of evidence that supports it.

Where once there were just one or two trainings offered in English only, there are now both specialty and comprehensive ADHD Coach training programs offered around the world in a variety of languages.

Where once there was no infrastructure to support ADHD Coaches, there is now an international professional association, an annual conference, an industry newsletter, an independent certifying and accrediting body, and online directories where people can find trained and experienced ADHD Coaches to help them, no matter where they live.

And yet there is still tremendous room for growth and maturation in the profession.

For example, there is nowhere near enough research on ADHD Coaching itself. We need to know exactly what the best practices and coaching models are, and we hope more researchers will find this a profitable area of study.

There are also nowhere near enough ADHD Coaches to help all those in need. ADHD affects roughly 5% of our population (the numbers in the scientific literature vary, but 5% is a defensible number). That means in the USA alone, there are roughly 15 million people who could benefit from working with an ADHD Coach. To meet that need, more training programs are offered every year by more and more teachers, and around the world more and more people are getting trained and certified as ADHD Coaches.

You can see that the field of ADHD Coaching is poised to take off.

Are you going to be part of it?

APPENDIX 1

ABOUT THE AUTHOR

Sarah D. Wright, MS, ACT, is an internationally known ADHD Coach, speaker, and author. Wright earned her BS from Stanford University, her MS from UNC Chapel Hill, her ADHD Coaching credential from the Optimal Functioning Institute, and her certificate for coaching ADHD youth from JST Coaching.

She is a founding board member of the ADHD Coaches Organization, where she served as president for many years, and was the 2012 recipient of the organization's award for *Distinguished Service to the Professional ADHD Coach Community.*

She is also a founding member of the ADHD Awareness Month Coalition, and co-founder of the San Diego-based coaching and consulting company, Focus For Effectiveness, LLC.

Wright served from 2008-2010 as the Executive Director of the Edge Foundation. It was under her tenure that the Edge Foundation conducted its pivotal study on the efficacy of ADHD Coaching on outcomes for college students with ADHD.

In addition to authoring this book, she is co-author of the popular book, *Fidget to Focus*, and contributing author to *365 Ways to Succeed with ADHD*, *365+1 Ways to Succeed with ADHD*, and *The ICD Guide to Collaborating with Professional Organizers*.

You can contact her at Sarah@SarahDWright.com.

APPENDIX 2

ABOUT THE ACO
& ACO BOOKS

The ADHD Coaches Organization is the professional association for ADHD Coaches. It is a not-for-profit 501(c)6 organization, founded in December 2005 to promote the profession of ADHD Coaching, to educate related professionals and the general public about the value of ADHD Coaching, and to support the growth and development of ADHD Coaches.

ACO Books is an imprint of the ADHD Coaches Organization. Its mission is to publish essential readings relevant to the profession of ADHD Coaching.

You can find out more about both the ACO and ACO Books on the web at ADHDCoaches.org.

APPENDIX 3

CHRONOLOGY OF THE DEVELOPMENT OF THE ACO

May 15, 2005   Tammy Cochrane and Glen Hogard give a presentation on the importance of forming an ADHD Coaches Association at the ADDA conference in Tucson, Arizona. A dozen or so coaches attended including Ken Zaretzky, Kerch McConlogue, Twila Gates, Kay Axtell, Kate Kelly, and Paul Ravenscraft.

May 30, 2005   The ADHDCoaches@yahoogroups.com list serve is created. Weekly teleconferences and steering committee meetings begin.

Jun 30, 2005   Ken Zaretzky articulates on the list serve what becomes the agreed-upon definition of what an ADHD Coach is: "It appears that there may be two schools of thought among us. I think there are some of us who see ADD coaches as a part of or an adjunct to the medical profession and a part of a medical team. Their training is generally medical and they may have some coach training. The other (which I fall on) appears to believe that an ADD Coach is a coach first. They are trained as a coach. They have special training, expertise or knowledge in addition to their coach training that qualifies them to specialize in working with people with Attention Deficit Disorder."

Jul 5, 2005	The list serve reaches 79 people. Participants include (in alphabetical order by last name): Linda Anderson, Denny Bausch, Deborah Bollom, Pat Bowton, Debra Bryan, Tammy Cochrane, Jan DeLaura, Ira Dressner, Judie Gade (Australia), Susan Gannon, Twila Gates, Holly Hamilton, John Hershey, Glen Hogard, Sharon Howell, Mary Jane Johnson, Donna Jaroslawski, Tereasa Jones, Jennifer Koretsky, Scott Lewis, Kerch McConlogue, Tara McGillicuddy, Harold Meyer, Lew Mills, Viveca Monahan, Gerard Montigny (Canada), Kris Paige, Rhonda Pawlan, Patti L. Petit, Dan Pruitt, Pete Quily (Canada), Linda Roggli, Judith Schwarcz (Israel), Jann Snyder, Terrence D. Sole, Leslie Vivian (Canada), Sarah D. Wright, and Ken Zaretzky.
Jul 13, 2005	The ADHD Coaches association officially becomes the "ADHD Coaches Organization."
Aug 31, 2005	The ACO website, ADHDCoaches.org, goes live.
Dec 16, 2005	Glen Hogard and Ken Zaretzky incorporate the ACO in New Mexico with the help of Cathy Jantzen.
Dec 21, 2005	The ACO holds its first board meeting and appoints its first Board of Directors: Cathy Jantzen President, Laurie Dupar Vice President, Sarah D. Wright Secretary, Jan DeLaura Treasurer, Ken Zaretzky Membership, Glen Hogard Marketing and PR, and Kerch McConlogue Communications.
Jan 1, 2006	The ACO begins accepting members.

Jan, 2006   The first issue of the ACO's monthly *Circle* newsletter is published. Kerch McConlogue is editor.

May 5 – 7, 2006   The ACO debuts at the ADDA Conference in Orlando, Florida and holds a membership drive. Membership tops 100.

May 4 – 6, 2006   The ACO holds its first international conference. One year after the idea was first floated, and 16 months after the ACO started accepting members, 40 coaches attend the first ever conference for ADHD Coaches in Chicago, Illinois. Kerch McConlogue is Conference Chair and Andrea Lee is keynote speaker.

Feb 20, 2007   The ACO is re-incorporated in Maryland.

Jun 1, 2007   The ACO implements its Leadership Team and the first team members, Gayla Wilson and Diane Ladd, take their positions.

Jan 2008   The ACO implements its Professional Advisory Board.

Feb 15, 2008   The ACO holds its first annual elections.

May 2 – 4, 2008   The ACO holds its second international conference. Fifty coaches attend the conference in St. Louis, Missouri. Kerch McConlogue is Conference Chair and Judith Kohlberg, founder of the organization now called The Institute for Challenging Disorganization, is keynote speaker.

Mar 2009   The ACO hires its first virtual assistant.

Apr 2009   The impact of the recession is felt everywhere, and the planned ACO conference is canceled for lack of enrollment.

Apr 30 – May 2, 2010   The ACO holds its third international conference. 75 coaches attend the conference in Chicago, Illinois. Viveca Monahan is Conference Chair and Russ Ramsay, PhD, is keynote speaker.

Dec 30, 2010   Membership tops 200.

Apr 30 – May 2, 2011   The ACO holds its fourth international conference. 108 coaches attend the conference in Chicago, Illinois. Viveca Monahan is Conference Chair and Gregg Krech, Director of the ToDo Institute, is keynote speaker. A celebration of life is held for Ken Zaretzky, co-founder of the ACO, who passed away on February 7, 2011. The ACO's inaugural award for *Distinguished Service to the Professional ADHD Coach Community* is presented to Glen Hogard for his seminal role in co-founding the ACO.

May 23 – 25, 2012   The ACO holds its fifth international conference. 132 coaches attend the conference in Atlanta, Georgia. Judith Champion is Conference Chair and Evelyn Green, President of ADDA, is keynote speaker. The ACO's award for *Distinguished Service to the Professional ADHD Coach Community* is presented to Sarah D. Wright, founding board member of the ACO, who served as president of the organization for five pivotal years.

Dec 31, 2012   Membership tops 300.

Apr 12 – 14,   The ACO holds its sixth international conference.
2013   137 coaches attend the conference in Atlanta, Georgia. Joyce Kubik is Conference Chair and Sari Solden is keynote speaker. A celebration of life is held for Kate Kelly, ADHD Coach and co-author of *You Mean I'm Not Lazy, Stupid or Crazy?!*, who passed away on September 13, 2012. The ACO's award for *Distinguished Service to the Professional ADHD Coach Community* is presented to Kerch McConlogue, founding board member of the ACO, for "having written or otherwise created everything everyone experiences as the ACO including the bylaws, the first strategic plan, the website, the annual conference which she chaired for two years, and the newsletter of which she was editor for five." The Thought Leader Summit is convened to help develop the definition of ADHD Coaching.

Dec 31, 2013   Membership tops 350.

May 2 – 4, 2014   The ACO holds its seventh international conference in Phoenix, Arizona. Katherine Jahnke and Robin Nordmeyer are Conference Co-Chairs and Laurie Dupar is keynote speaker. The ACO's award for *Distinguished Service to the Professional ADHD Coach Community* is awarded to Madelyn Griffith-Haynie, co-founder of the ADHD Coaching profession.

APPENDIX 4

CHRONOLOGY OF THE DEVELOPMENT OF ADHD COACHING

1971   Werner Erhard establishes EST Training at Esalen, which became The Forum and then Landmark Education.

1974   *The Inner Game of Tennis* by Timothy Gallwey is published.

1981   Thomas Leonard starts working as the Budget Director for Landmark Education.

1988   Thomas Leonard develops his *Design Your Life* course.

1992   Thomas Leonard founds CoachU. Laura Whitworth co-founds the Coach Training Institute (CTI).

1993   *You Mean I'm not Lazy, Stupid or Crazy?!* by Kate Kelly and Peggy Ramundo is published.

1994   *Driven to Distraction* by Ned Hallowell and John Ratey is published. Madelyn Griffith-Haynie, a student of Thomas Leonard, founds the Optimal Functioning Institute (OFI). Nancy Ratey and Sue Sussman found the National Coaching Network (NCN). Thomas Leonard founds the International Coach Federation (ICF).

1995   Laura Whitworth and colleagues found the
        Professional and Personal Coaches Association
        (PPCA).

1996   Thomas Leonard sells CoachU to Sandy Vilas and
        leaves ICF.

1997   Ben Dean founds MentorCoach.

1998   Pat Williams founds The Institute for Life Coach
        Training (ILCT). National Coaching Network
        becomes the American Coaching Association
        (ACA). David Giwerc founds the ADD Coach
        Academy (ADDCA).The PPCA is folded into ICF;
        ICF becomes the organization it is today.

2000   Association of Coach Training Organizations (ACTO)
        formed to promote and support the evolution of
        quality coach training.

2001   Thomas Leonard launches Coachville and the
        Graduate School of Coaching.

2002   ADDA develops and publishes guidelines for ADHD
        Coaching edited by Nancy Ratey and Peter Jaska.

2003   Thomas Leonard passes away. International
        Association of Coaching (IAC) launched. CHADD
        publishes guidelines for ADHD Coaching, modeled
        after ADDA's 2002 guidelines.

2004   Jodi Sleeper-Triplett starts JST ADHD Youth Coach
        Training Program.

2005   Institute for Advancement of ADHD Coaching (IAAC) is founded. ADHD Coaches Organization (ACO) is founded.

2007   The first ACO International Conference for ADHD Coaches is held in Chicago, Illinois.

2009   Professional Association of ADHD Coaches (PAAC) is founded.

2011   Pat Williams collaborates with CCE to launch the Board Certified Coach (BCC) certification.

2013   Institute for Advancement of ADHD Coaching (IAAC) dissolved. ACO hosts the Thought Leader Summit leading to the definition of ADHD Coaching.

NOTES

Preface

1. Edward Hallowell and John Ratey, *Driven to Distraction* (NY: Pantheon Books, 1994).

2. Kate Kelly and Peggy Ramundo, *You Mean I'm Not Lazy, Stupid or Crazy?!* (Cincinnati: Tyrell & Jerem Press, 1993).

Chapter 1

3. Vicki Brock, *Sourcebook of Coaching History* (CreateSpace, 2012).

Chapter 2

4. Sandy Maynard, "Personal and Professional Coaching: A Literature Review," 2006; Vicki Brock, *Sourcebook of Coaching History* (CreateSpace, 2012).

5. Vicki Brock, "Grounded Theory of the Roots and Emergence of Coaching," 2008. This is Brock's dissertation. It can be found online at http://libraryofprofessionalcoaching.com/wp-app/wpcontent/ uploads/2011/10/dissertation.pdf.

6. W. Timothy Gallwey, *The Inner Game of Tennis* (New York: Random House, 1974).

7. Joseph O'Connor and Andrea Lages, *How Coaching Works: The Essential Guide to the History and Practice of Effective Coaching* (London: A&C Black, 2007), 23-24. This book is available as a downloadable pdf at http://103.9.88.89/app/2013-11-23/How_Coaching_ Works_1.pdf.

8. Vicki Brock, *Sourcebook of Coaching History* (CreateSpace, 2012). Brock's book is based on her 2008 dissertation, "Grounded Theory of the Roots and Emergence of Coaching."

9. O'Connor and Lages, *How Coaching Works*, 25.

10. Ibid., 26; Madelyn Griffith-Haynie, Personal Communication, 2014.

11. O'Connor and Lages, *How Coaching Works*, 26.

12. Nancy Ratey, Personal Communication, 2014; C.J. Hayden, Personal Communication, 2014.

13. Ratey, Personal Communication; Hayden, Personal Communication; Brock, "Grounded Theory."

14. Brock, "Grounded Theory," 266-267.

15. Madelyn Griffith-Haynie, Personal Communication, 2014.

16. O'Connor and Lages, *How Coaching Works*, 26; Hayden, Personal Communication, 2014; David Matthew Prior, Personal Communication, 2014.

17. The two largest European life coach certification organizations are the European Mentoring & Coaching Council (EMCC), co-founded in 1992 by Eric Parsloe, David Megginson, David Clutterbuck, and Sir John Whitmore among others, which as of the publication of this book has over 5,000 members in 67 countries (http://www. emccouncil.org/), and the International Coaching Community (ICC), founded in 2001 by Joseph O'Connor and Andrea Lages, which as of publication has over 8000 certified Coaches in 60 countries (http:// www.internationalcoachingcommunity.com/). These organizations are mentioned here rather than in the text, as there are currently no ACO members certified by either organization, and the overlap of these organizations with ADHD Coaching appears minimal.

18. Edward Hallowell and John Ratey, *Driven to Distraction* (NY: Pantheon Books,1994), 225-227.

Chapter 3

19. Griffith-Haynie, Personal Communication, 2014.

20. Ratey, Personal Communication, 2014.

21. Ratey, Personal Communication, 2014.

22. Lisa Grossman, Personal Communication, 2014.

23. Sue Sussman, Personal Communication, 2013.

24. Nancy Ratey and Peter Jaska, editors, "The ADDA Guiding Principles for Coaching Individuals with Attention Deficit Disorder," 2002.

25. Ibid.

26. "Coaching for Adults with ADHD (WWK18)," CHADD. http://www help4adhd.org/en/living/coaching/WWK18/

27. http://www.paaccoaches.org/mission-vision/

Chapter 4

28. Margaret Moore et al., "Fundamentals of Coaching Psychology," in *Coaching Psychology Manual* (Baltimore: Lippincott Williams & Wilkins, 2010).

29. Moore, "Fundamentals of Coaching Psychology."

30. Dianne R Stober and Anthony M Grant, *Evidence Based Coaching Handbook: Putting Best Practices to Work for Your Clients* (Hoboken: John Wiley & Sons, 2006), 2; Carol Kauffman, "From Clinical to Positive Psychology: My journey to Coaching," in *How Coaching Works: The Essential Guide to the History and Practice of Effective Coaching* (London: A&C Black, 2007), 123.

31. Robert Dilts, "NLP and Coaching with a Capital 'C'," in *How Coaching Works: The Essential Guide to the History and Practice of Effective Coaching* (London: A&C Black, 2007), 105.

32. Christina A Douglas and Cynthia D McCauley, "Formal developmental relationships: A survey of organizational practices," 1999.

33. Robert Dilts, "NLP and Coaching with a Capital 'C'," 105.

34. American Psychiatric Association, *Diagnostic and statistical manual of mental disorders 5th Edition*, 2013.

35. Dianne R Stober and Anthony M Grant, *Evidence Based Coaching Handbook: Putting Best Practices to Work for Your Clients* (Hoboken: John Wiley & Sons, 2006), 2; O'Connor and Lages, *How Coaching Works*, 16; Nancy Ratey, *The Disorganized Mind: Coaching Your ADHD Brain to Take Control of Your Time, Tasks, and Talents* (New York: St. Martin's Griffin, 2008), 18.

Chapter 5

36. Sam Goldstein, "Editorial: Coaching as a Treatment for ADHD," 2005.

37. Christina A Douglas and Cynthia D McCauley, "Formal developmental relationships: A survey of organizational practices," 1999.

38. Robert Dilts, "NLP and Coaching with a Capital 'C'," in *How Coaching Works: The Essential Guide to the History and Practice of Effective Coaching* (London: A&C Black, 2007), 105.

39. Jeffrey E Auerbach, "Cognitive Coaching," in *Evidence Based Coaching Handbook* (Hoboken: John Wiley & Sons, 2006).

40. Carol Kauffman, "Positive Psychology: The Science at the Heart of Coaching," in *Evidence Based Coaching Handbook*; Robert Biswas-Deiner, *Practicing Positive Psychology Coaching* (Hoboken: John Wiley & Sons, 2010).

41. Ari Tuckman, *Integrative Treatment for Adult ADHD: A Practical, Easy-To-Use Guide for Clinicians* (Oakland: New Harbinger Publications, 2007), 189.

42. Russell Barkley, "Executive Functioning in ADHD: Implications for Assessment and Management," 2012.

43. Robert Dilts, "NLP and Coaching with a Capital 'C'," 105.

44. Peg Dawson and Richard Guare, *Coaching Students with Executive Skills Deficits* (NY: Guilford Press, 2012).

45. Hallowell and Ratey, *Driven to Distraction*, 225-227.

46. Tuckman, *Integrative Treatment for Adult ADHD*, 189.

47 Elaine Cox, "An Adult Learning Approach to Coaching," in *Evidence Based Coaching Handbook* (Hoboken: John Wiley & Sons, 2006).

48. Steven A Safren et al., *Mastering Your Adult ADHD* (NY: Oxford University Press, 2005).

49. Russell Barkley, "Executive Functioning in ADHD: Implications for Assessment and Management," 2012.

50. Russell Barkley, Personal Communication, 2012.

51. RV Estrada et al., "Psychoeducation for adults with Attention Deficit Hyperactivity Disorder vs. cognitive behavioral group therapy: a randomized controlled pilot study," 2013.

52. Kelly and Ramundo, *You Mean I'm Not Lazy, Stupid or Crazy?!*.

53. Maite Ferrin et al., "Evaluation of a psychoeducation programme for parents of children and adolescents with ADHD: immediate and long-term effects using a blind randomized controlled trial," 2013. Available online at http://www.ncbi.nlm.nih.gov/pubmed/24292412.

54. Tuckman, *Integrative Treatment for Adult ADHD*; Estrada et al., "Psychoeducation," 2013; Ferrin et al., "Evaluation," 2013.

55. Safren et al., *Mastering Your Adult ADHD*; Auerbach, "Cognitive Coaching," in *Evidence Based Coaching Handbook*; Cox, "An Adult Learning Approach to Coaching," in *Evidence Based Coaching Handbook*; Grant, "An Integrative Goal-Focused Approach to Executive

Coaching" in *Evidence Based Coaching Handbook*; Kauffman, "Positive Psychology: The Science at the Heart of Coaching," in *Evidence Based Coaching Handbook*; David B Peterson, "People are Complex and the World is Messy: A Behavior-Based Approach to Executive Coaching" in *Evidence Based Coaching Handbook*; Dianne R Stober, "Coaching from the Humanistic Perspective" in *Evidence Based Coaching Handbook* (Hoboken: John Wiley & Sons, 2006); Tuckman, *Integrative Treatment for Adult ADHD*; Biswas-Deiner, *Practicing Positive Psychology Coaching*; Barkley, "Executive Functioning in ADHD."

56. Stober and Grant, *Evidence Based Coaching Handbook*; Kauffman, "From Clinical to Positive Psychology," 2007), 123; Margaret Moore et al., "Fundamentals of Coaching Psychology," in *Coaching Psychology Manual* (Baltimore: Lippincott Williams & Wilkins, 2010).

57. David Parker and Karen Boutelle, "Executive Function Coaching for College Students with LD and ADHD: A New Approach for Fostering Self-Determination," 2009; Kubik, "Efficacy of ADHD Coaching for Adults With ADHD," 2010; David Parker et al., "An Examination of the Effects of ADHD Coaching on University Students' Executive Functioning," 2011; David Parker et al., "Self-control in postsecondary settings: Students' perceptions of ADHD college coaching," 2012; Sharon Field et al., "Assessing the impact of ADHD Coaching Services on University Students' Learning Skills, Self-Regulation, and Well-Being," 2013; Frances Prevatt and Sherry Yelland, "An Empirical Evaluation of ADHD Coaching in College Students," 2013.

Chapter 6

58. Kubik, "Efficacy of ADHD Coaching."

Chapter 7

59. International Coach Federation, "Background Information & Membership Facts—March 2014."

Chapter 8

60. Professional Association of ADHD Coaches Mission & Vision, http://www.paaccoaches.org/mission-vision/.

GLOSSARY

AAC   ADDCA Associate Coach, designates graduation from the Basic ADHD Coach Training Program at the ADD Coach Academy (ADDCA)

AACC   ADDCA Associate Certified Coach, basic certification from the ADD Coach Academy (ADDCA)

ACA   American Coaching Association, on the web at americoach.org

ACAC   Associate Certified ADHD Coach, basic certification from the Institute for the Advancement of ADHD Coaching (IAAC)

ACC   Associate Certified Coach, basic certification from the International Coach Federation (ICF)

ACCG   ADDCA Certified Coach Graduate, advanced certification from the ADD Coach Academy (ADDCA)

ACG   ADDCA Coach Graduate, designates graduation from the Advanced ADHD Coach Training Program at the ADD Coach Academy (ADDCA)

ACO   ADHD Coaches Organization, on the web at adhdcoaches.org

ACSTH	Approved Coach Specific Training Hours from the International Coach Federation (ICF)
AACSTH	Approved ADHD Coach Specific Training Hours from the Professional Association of ADHD Coaches (PAAC)
ACT	ADHD Coach Training, certification from the Optimal Functioning Institute (OFI)
ACTO	Association of Coach Training Organizations, on the web at actoonline.org
ACTP	Approved Coach Training Program from the International Coach Federation (ICF)
AACTP	Approved ADHD Coach Training Program from the Professional Association of ADHD Coaches (PAAC)
ADDA	Attention Deficit Disorder Association, on the web at add.org
ADDCA	ADD Coach Academy, on the web at addcoachacademy.com
ASCT	ADD in the Spirit Coach Training, on the web at addcoaching.com
BCC	Board Certified Coach, certification from the Center for Credentialing and Education (CCE)

CAC   Certified ADHD Coach, intermediate certification
from the Institute for the Advancement of ADHD
Coaching (IAAC)

CAC   Certified ADHD Coach, basic certification from
Impact Coaching Academy (ICA)

CACEU   Continuing ADHD Coach Education Units from the
Professional Association of ADHD Coaches (PAAC)

CACP   Certified ADHD Coach Practitioner, basic
certification from the Professional Association of
ADHD Coaches (PAAC)

CAOC   Certified ADHD Organizer Coach, certification from
the Coach Approach for Organizers

CCE   Center for Credentialing and Education, on the web
at cce-global.org

CCE   Continuing Coach Education from the International
Coach Federation (ICF)

CCEU   An acronym used in this book to stand for Continuing
Coach Education Units and to distinguish ICF
Continuing Coach Education from the Center for
Credentialing and Education.

CHADD   Children and Adults with ADHD, on the web at
chadd.org

CMAC   Certified Master ADHD Coach, advanced certification from Impact Coaching Academy (ICA)

CMC   Certified MentorCoach, certification from MentorCoach

CMC   Certified Masteries Coach, basic certification from the International Association of Coaching (IAC)

COC   Certified Organizer Coach, certification from the Coach Approach for Organizers

COLC   Certified Organizer Life Coach, certification from the Coach Approach for Organizers

CPCC   Certified Professional Co-Active Coach, certification from the Coach Training Institute (CTI)

CPLC   Certified Productivity Leadership Coach, certification from the Coach Approach for Organizers

CPO   Certified Professional Organizer, certification from the National Association of Professional Organizers (NAPO)

CPO-CD Certified Professional Organizer - Challenging Disorganization, certification from the Institute for Challenging Disorganization (ICD)

CSS   Career Services Specialist, certification from the Edge Foundation's continuing coach education program

CSST   Career Services Specialty Training, the web at
        edgefoundation.org/cceu

 CTI   Coach Training Institute, on the web at
        thecoaches.com

IAAC   Institute for the Advancement of ADHD Coaching
        (no longer in operation)

 IAC   International Association of Coaching, on the web at
        certifiedcoach.org

 ICA   Impact Coaching Academy, on the web at
        impactcoachingacademy.com

 ICD   Institute for Challenging Disorganization, on the web
        at challengingdisorganization.org

 ICF   International Coach Federation, on the web at
        coachfederation.org

ILCT   The Institute for Life Coach Training, on the web at
        lifecoachtraining.com

MCAC   Master Certified ADHD Coach, advanced
        certification from the Professional Association of
        ADHD Coaches (PAAC)

 MCC   Master Certified Coach, advanced certification from
        the International Coach Federation (ICF)

 MMC   Master Masteries Coach, advanced certification
        from the International Association of Coaching (IAC)

NAPO   National Association of Professional Organizers, on the web at napo.net

NCN   National Coaching Network, (no longer in operation, subsumed into ACA)

OFI   Optimal Functioning Institute, on the web at addcoach.com

PAAC   Professional Association of ADHD Coaches, on the web at paaccoaches.org

PACG   Professional ADDCA Coach Graduate, designates graduation from the Professional Advanced ADHD Coach Training Program at the ADD Coach Academy (ADDCA)

PCAC   Professional Certified ADHD Coach, intermediate certification from the Professional Association of ADHD Coaches (PAAC)

PCC   Professional Certified Coach, intermediate certification from the International Coach Federation (ICF)

PPCA   Professional and Personal Coaches Association (no longer in operation, subsumed into ICF)

SCAC   Senior Certified ADHD Coach, advanced certification from the Institute for the Advancement of ADHD Coaching (IAAC)

BIBLIOGRAPHY

ADDA. "The ADDA Guiding Principles for Coaching Individuals with Attention Deficit Disorder." *NancyRatey.com*. 2002. http://www. nancyratey.com/adhdcoaching/adda- coachingprinciples (accessed March 15, 2014).

American Psychiatric Association. *Diagnostic and statistical manual of mental disorders*. 5th. Arlington, VA: American Psychiatric Publishing, 2013.

Auerbach, Jeffrey E. "Cognitive Coaching." In *Evidence Based Coaching Handbook*, by Dianne R Stober and Anthony M Grant, 103-127. Hoboken, NJ: John Wiley and Sons, 2006.

Barkley, Russell. "Executive Functioning in ADHD: Implications for Assessment and Management." *CHADD Preconference Institute*. 2012.

Barkley, Russell, interview by Sarah D. Wright. *Personal Communication* (December 4, 2012).

Biswas-Deiner, Robert. *Practicing Positive Psychology Coaching*. Hoboken, NJ: John Wiley and Sons, 2010.

Brock, Vikki G. *Grounded Theory of the Roots and Emergence of Coaching*. Doctoral Dissertation, Coaching and Human Development, International University of Professional Studies, http:// libraryofprofessionalcoaching.com, 2008.

—. *Sourcebook of Coaching History*. Create Space, 2012.

CHADD. "Coaching for Adults with ADHD (WWK18)." *National Resource Center on ADHD - a Program of CHADD*. 2003. http://www.help4adhd. org/en/living/coaching/WWK18/ (accessed March 15, 2014).

Cox, Elaine. "An Adult learning Approach to Coaching." In *Evidence Based Coaching Handbook*, by Dianne R Stober and Anthony M Grant, 193-218. Hoboken, NJ: John Wiley and Sons, 2006.

Dawson, Peg, and Richard Guare. *Coaching Students with Executive Skills Deficits*. New York: Guilford Press, 2012.

Dilts, R. "NLP and Coaching with a Capital 'C'." In *How Coaching Works: The Essential Guide to the History and Practice of Effective Coaching*, by J., and Lages, A. O'Connor, 275. London: A&C Black, 2007.

Douglas, Christina A, and Cynthia D McCauley. "Formal developmental relationships: A survey of organizational practices." *Human Resource Development Quarterly* 10, no. 3 (1999): 203-220.

Estrada, RV, et al. "Psychoeducation for adults with Attention Deficit Hyperactivity Disorder vs. cognitive behavioral group therapy: a randomized controlled pilot study." *The Journal of Nervous and Mental Disease* 201, no. 10 (October 2013): 894-9000.

Ferrin, M, JM Moreno-Granados, MD Salcedo-Marin, M Ruiz-Veguilla, V Perez-Ayala, and E Taylor. "Evaluation of a psychoeducation programme for parents of children and adolescents with ADHD: immediate and long-term effects using a blind randomized controlled trial." *European Child and Adolescent Psychiatry*, Dec 2013.

Field, Sharon, David R Parker, Shlomo Sawilowsky, and Laura Rolands. "Assessing the impact of ADHD Coaching Services on University

Students' Learning Skills, Self- Regulation, and Well-Being." *Journal of Postsecondary Education and Disability* (AHEAD) 26, no. 1 (2013): 67-81.

Gallwey, W. Timothy. *The Inner Game of Tennis*. New York, NY: Random House, 1974.

Goldstein, S. "Editorial: Coaching as a Treatment for ADHD." *Journal of Attention Disorders* 9, no. 2 (Nov 2005): 379-381.

Grant, Anthony M. "An Integrative Goal-Focused Approach to Executive Coaching." In *Evidence Based Coaching Handbook*, by Dianne R Stober and Anthony M Grant, 153-192. Hoboken, NJ: John Wiley and Sons, 2006.

Griffith-Haynie, interview by Sarah D. Wright *Personal Communication* (April 7, 2014).

Grossman, Lisa, interview by Sarah D. Wright. *Personal Communication* (March 20, 2014).

Hallowell, Edward, and John Ratey. *Driven To Distraction: Recognizing and Coping with Attention Deficit Disorder from Childhood Through Adulthood*. New York, NY: Pantheon Books, 1994.

Hayden, C.J., interview by Sarah D. Wright. *Personal Communication* (March 15, 2014).

International Coach Federation. *Background Information & Membership Facts—March 2014*. Marketing Department , International Coach Federation, International Coach Federation, 2014.

Kauffman, Carol. "From Clinical to Positive Psychology: My journey to Coaching." In *How Coaching Works: The Essential Guide to the History and Practice of Effective Coaching*, by Joseph O'Connor and Andrea Lages. London: A & C Black, 2007.

—. "Positive Psychology: The Science at the Heart of Coaching." In *Evidence Based Coaching Handbook*, by Dianne R Stober and Anthony M Grant, 219-254. Hoboken, NJ: John Wiley and Sons, 2006.

Kelly, Kate, and Peggy Ramundo. *You Mean I'm Not Lazy, Stupid or Crazy?!* Cincinnati, OH: Tyrell & Jerem Press, 1993.

Kubik, Joyce A. "Efficacy of ADHD Coaching for Adults With ADHD." *Journal of Attention Disorders* (Sage Publications) 13 (March 2010): 442-453.

Maynard, Sandy. "Personal and Professional Coaching: A Literature Review." Masters Thesis, Psychology , Walden University , 2006.

Moore, Margaret, Bob Tschannen-Moran, Gloria Silverio, and Lori Gray Boothroyd. "Fundamentals of Coaching Psychology." In *Coaching Psychology Manual*, by Margaret Moore and Bob Tschannen-Moran, 3-16. Baltimore, MD: Lippincott Williams & Wilkins, 2010.

O'Connor, Joseph, and Andrea Lages. *How Coaching Works: The Essential Guide to the History and Practice of Effective Coaching*. London: A&C Black, 2007.

Parker, David R., and Karen Boutelle. "Executive Function Coaching for College Students with LD and ADHD: A New Approach for Fostering Self-Determination." *Learning Disabilities Research & Practice* 24, no. 4 (2009): 204-215.

Parker, David R., Sharon Field Hoffman, Shlomo Sawilowsky, and Laura Rolands. "An Examination of the Effects of ADHD Coaching on University Students' Executive Functioning." *Journal of Postsecondary Education and Disability* 24, no. 2 (2011): 115-132.

Parker, David R., Sharon Field, Schlomo Sawilowsky, and Laura Rolands. "Self-control in postsecondary settings: Students' perceptions of ADHD college coaching." *Journal of Attention Disorders* 26, no. 1 (2012): 67-81.

Peterson, David B. "People are Complex and the World is Messy: A Behavior-Based Approach to Executive Coaching." In *Evidence Based Coaching Handbook*, by Dianne R Stober and Anthony M Grant, 51-76. 51-76, NJ: John Wiley and Sons, 2006.

Prevatt, Frances, and Sherry Yelland. "An Empirical Evaluation of ADHD Coaching in College Students." *Journal of Attention Disorders* (Sage Publications), 3 2013: 1-12.

Prior, David, interview by Sarah D. Wright. *Personal Communication* (March 20, 2014).

Professional Association of ADHD Coaches. *PAAC Mission/Vision.* http://www.paaccoaches.org/mission-vision/ (accessed March 15, 2014).

Ratey, Nancy, interview by Sarah D. Wright. *Personal Communication* (March 20, 2014).

—. *The Disorganized Mind: Coaching Your ADHD Brain to Take Control of Your Time, Tasks, and Talents*. New York, NY: St. Martin's Griffin, 2008.

Safren, Steven A, Susan Sprich, Carol A Perlman, and Michael W Otto. *Mastering Your Adult ADHD*. New York: Oxford University Press, 2005.

Stober, Dianne R. "Coaching from the Humanistic Perspective." In *Evidence Based Coaching Handbook*, by Dianne R Stober and Anthony M Grant, 17-50. Hoboken, NJ: John Wiley and Sons, 2006.

Stober, Dianne R, and Anthony M Grant. *Evidence Based Coaching Handbook: Putting Best Practices to Work for Your Clients*. Hoboken, NJ: John Wiley & Sons, 2006.

Sussman, Sue, interview by Sarah D. Wright. *Personal Communication* (April 10, 2013).

Tuckman, Ari. *Integrative Treatment for Adult ADHD: A Practical, Easy-To-Use Guide for Clinicians*. Oakland, CA: New Harbinger Publications, 2007.

INDEX

A

I

J

K

L

M

N

O

P

V

Volio, Lupita, 12, 62

W

Whitworth, Laura, 6, appendix 4

Williams, Pat, 8-9, 16, 80, appendix 4

Wright, Sarah D., 15

Z

Zaretzky, Ken, 15, appendix 3

Made in the USA
Lexington, KY
26 January 2015